GETTI

MW01039351

PERSONAL

GETTING
PERSONAL

FEMINIST

OCCASIONS

AND

OTHER

AUTOBIOGRAPHICAL ACTS

NANCY K. MILLER

Routledge · New York & London

Published in 1991 by

Routledge
An imprint of Routledge, Chapman and Hall, Inc.
29 West 35 Street
New York, NY 10001

Published in Great Britain by

Routledge
11 New Fetter Lane
London EC4P 4EE

Printed in the United States of America

Library of Congress Cataloging in Publication Data

Miller, Nancy K.
    Getting personal : feminist occasions and other
autobiographical acts / Nancy K. Miller.
        p.   cm.
    Includes bibliographical references and index.
    ISBN 0-415-90323-8 (HB).—ISBN 0-415-90324-6 (PB)
    1. Feminist literary criticism.   2. Feminism and literature.
3. Women and literature.   4. Autobiography.   I. Title.
PN98.W64M55   1991
801'.95'082—dc20   91-7404
                                                              CIP

British Library Cataloguing in Publication Data also available.

In Memoriam

LK

Contents

. . . and Occasions

(Chapters 1–8 variously originated in talks and lectures. I
gratefully acknowledge here these occasions.—NKM)

1. "What Is an Author?" Interdisciplinary Seminar, Cambridge University, England (1990)
2. "The Scholar and the Feminist V: Creating Feminist Works," Conference, Barnard College Women's Center, New York, New York (1978)
3. "Feminist Pedagogy: Positions and Points of View," MLA, Houston, Texas (1980). "Reading the Two Georges: Sand, Eliot, and the Making of Feminist Canons," MLA, New Orleans, Louisiana (1988)
4. "Français impeccable: Memoirs of a Near Native Speaker," MLA, New Orleans, Louisiana (1988)
5. "Do Women's Studies Make a Difference?" Roundtable, Wesleyan University, Middletown, Connecticut (1986)
6. "Feminism and the Dream of a Plural Culture," Conference, Queens College, New York (1988). Colloquium, The School of Criticism and Theory, Dartmouth College, Hanover, New Hampshire (1988)
7. "Conference on Narrative Literature," University of Wisconsin, Madison, Wisconsin (1989). "Double Trouble: The Subject in Feminism," Conference, University of Utrecht, Holland (1990)
8. "The Subject of Autobiography," Conference, University of Southern Maine, Portland, Maine (1989)

Preface

Feminist Confessions:
The Last Degrees Are the Hardest

[handwritten margin note: labels in clothing attached to a man-aquin]

In a reading group I belonged to in the mid-eighties, we talked on and off about the liabilities that attached to the transfer of the adjective "feminist" from a political movement to a critical label. One of the women in the group objected hotly to receiving professional invitations to speak "as a feminist" at conferences and campuses. She wanted, she said, to be invited for herself, as "a critic"—minus any label or constituency; and mimed the dismay of the generic departmental host, who finding himself saddled with the feminist speaker imported to his campus for the occasion, attempts to naturalize the event and banish discomfort in his role by being humorous: "Why don't we go have some feminist ice cream," he chortles, "ho, ho, ho." I understood perfectly what she meant, but at the same time, I found myself stuck on the very point. Who would I be on those occasions, if not the "feminist" speaker?

In the last couple of years, I have begun to ponder the implications of that critic's revolt against the feminist label. Not because I resent the label's application to my work, or feel intellectually reduced by feminism's engagements, but because the resistance she expresses to a *position of representativity* bears a certain kinship, I think, to two distinct phenomena that have emerged together on the critical horizon over the decade of the eighties—albeit on separate tracks. The first (although it is not practiced uniquely by feminists or women) can be seen to develop out of feminist theory's original emphasis on the analysis of the personal: I'm referring to the current proliferation in literary studies of autobiographical or personal criticism. (I'll distinguish between these two terms in Chapter 1 below.) This outbreak of self-writing, which may be interpreted, no doubt, as one of the many symptoms of literary theory's mid-life crisis, also intersects with a certain overloading in cultural criticism of the rhetorics of representativity (including feminism's)—the incantatory recital of the "speaking as a"s and the imperialisms of "speaking for"s. I read this work as a renewed attention to the unidentified voices of a writing self outside or to the side of labels, or at least at a critical distance from them, and at the same time as part of a wider effort to remap the theoretical. The spectacle of a significant number of critics getting personal in their writing, while not, to be sure, on the order of a paradigm shift, is at least the sign of a turning point in the history of critical practices.

The other development is a visible trend (important enough for the MLA Commission on the Status of Women to take it up as an issue) of attacks on academic feminism—a kind of critical misogyny practiced by women as well as men—that has been cropping up (along with gay bashing) in a variety of institutional contexts and guises.[1] What should we make of this published violence against feminist ideology in general and individual critics in particular (ad feminam)? One could of course take the fatalistic view that every critical movement has its allotted life span in academia and is meant to be superseded: the new criticism is now old, structuralism is post, why not also feminism? Or the Old Testament line that since feminism as a mode of critique began by attacking other positions, why shouldn't it get attacked back (a version of childhood cries of injustice: she started it)? Or maybe it's simply the case that feminism is now seen to be powerful enough to inspire the kinds of resentments that any configuration perceived to be "overrepresented" is thought to deserve?[2]

One might also take the longer and more productive view that feminism needs to be self-critical in order to evolve, and that these volleys offer an occasion to reexamine the assumptions of its operations. The dislocations within feminism, moreover—the refusal of a hegemonic and unitary feminism—have already instituted this process. In this sense, I would argue, representativity is a problem *within* feminism itself: a matter of self-representation and as such the subject of this book.

The individual "I":

Feminist Confessions

The occasions I record here are thus both scenes of feminism— *problems*
conferences (at Barnard, Queens, Utrecht) or academic meetings
(MLA) devoted self-consciously to these questions—and texts (cri- *question*
tiques) *for* feminism. But by feminist occasions I also mean events not
specifically marked off by the label—like the conferences on narrative
and on autobiography or the seminar on authorship—which by their
intellectual spaciousness provided the room in which to deal freely
with these questions. *and ethnography*

Most of the chapters of this book were, at least originally, occasional.
I have never really understood why occasional writing is held to be a
deconsidered genre (especially by editors and reviewers) and why,
therefore, the traces of the event that so often have informed—not to
say occasioned—the writing for them are just as often erased.[3] (Actually, I do understand, but I don't share the prejudice. I prefer the
gossipy grain of situated writing to the academic sublime.) The scenes
in which academics and critics perform (however domesticated they
might seem to become—even the MLA, after the initial shock wears
off) are constrained by institutional protocols more rigid in some ways
than those that regulate the classroom. They are worth attending to.

What interests me in the juncture of essay and academic event is the
effect of the local contexts of work—even if with time (and revision)
the reader, like the writer, is necessarily left with a paper occasion.
Academic events shape critical practices trans-institutionally and publicly, and need to remain a visible part of both the writing and our
discussions of it.[4] In some cases, this recognition may require merely a
locational marker; in others, especially in the stormy history of feminist
theory, we need entire conference narratives: a potential academic sub-
genre.[5]

In the folds of this book, practicing a version of autobiographical
writing I call narrative criticism, I try to delineate the political stakes
of these occasions, at least as I see them, for the annals of feminism.
But more locally, and I guess more selfishly, in the notion of the
occasional I have also wanted to seize the fallout of event: the
chance for something to happen in the wedge of unpredictability

xi

not yet foreclosed by my own (rhetorically predictable) feminist discourse.

I call the earliest piece of this book "Untitled Work" because its only name was a generic one: the name of a panel, "Creating Feminist Works," that was the plenary session in 1978 of an annual event held at Barnard College, a conference called "The Scholar and the Feminist." In the discussion period, I was asked a question about my use of metaphors: did I really mean that like onions, women's texts had "no core" (unlike men's which had artichoke hearts)? I answered then (defensively, as I tend to do when challenged in public), that metaphors (meaning mine) probably shouldn't be taken too seriously. But metaphors are to be taken very seriously, and they still appeal to me as an economical way both to theorize outside of systems dependent on a unitary signature (allowing you to combine things that usually don't go together) and to imagine in the material of language what hasn't yet come—what might not be able to come—into social being. Although I of course do not make the claim that the use of metaphor in critical theory is specifically (essentially) feminist, I do think that metaphor, which as a figure involves a movement (displacement, transfer) of meaning, has been particularly productive for feminist utopian thought.[6] In my own work, I have been especially attracted to the expansion of metaphor into allegory or fable like the one here of Philoctetes' island. Perhaps what seems most "feminist" to me about the uses of both metaphor and narrative criticism is the self-consciousness these modes of analysis tend to display about their own processes of theorization; a self-consciousness that points to the fictional strategies inherent in all theory.

Like "Untitled Work," several chapters turn around questions of teaching. All deal in different ways with issues of representativity (the "as a" problem): teaching as a feminist. They all also address dilemmas of authority and mastery—feminism "vs." theory—and, especially in the case of graduate teaching, the question of what one's responsibility as a feminist and a teacher is to students who want to become feminist critics. These pieces therefore dwell on positionings, modelings, and the irreducible ambiguity of those postures for feminist pedagogy.

In 1980, a few days before he died, Roland Barthes gave an interview that was published in *Le Nouvel Observateur* under the title "The Crisis of Desire." Invited to comment on the new conformity and the failure of all protest movements in France, Barthes remarks that "the only effective marginalism is individualism."[7] He then goes on to make the claim, not fully worked out, that this individualism—refashioned— could be understood as radical and not a return to a petit-bourgeois liberalism. Barthes writes: "The mere fact, for instance, of thinking my body until I reach the point at which I know that I can think *only* my body is an attitude that comes up against science, fashion, morality, all collectivities" (85). The language of his thinking here intersects unexpectedly with Adrienne Rich's body prose in "Notes for a Politics of Location." Rich writes: "Perhaps we need a moratorium on saying 'the body.' For it's also possible to abstract 'the' body. When I write 'the body,' I see nothing in particular. To write 'my body' plunges me into lived experience, particularity. . . . To say 'the body' lifts me away from what has given me a primary perspective. To say 'my body' reduces the temptation to grandiose assertions" (215). Rich's commitment to the political, to militancy, to the collective; Barthes's complete resistance to all of the above: "I've never been a militant and it would be impossible for me to be one for personal reasons I have about language: I don't like militant language" (86): despite the gulf separating their views of the intellectual's role in cultural criticism, what joins them, I think, is the sense they share of the ways in which one's own body can constitute an internal limit on discursive irresponsibility, a brake on rhetorical spinning. The autobiographical act—however self-fictional, can like the detail of one's (aging) body, produce this sense of limit as well: the resistance particularity offers to the grandiosity of abstraction that inhabits what I've been calling the crisis of representativity.[8] (Perhaps we also need a moratorium on *reciting the litany* of RaceClassGender and instead a rush into *doing* positive things with those words.[9])

Both Barthes's last words about individualism and the inward focus of autobiographical writing present obvious problems for a social, affirmative activism in which—"as a feminist"—I still believe. In the face of the visible extremes of racism or misogyny, or the equally violent silences of theoretical discourses from which all traces of embodiment have been carefully abstracted, the autobiographical project might seem a frivolous response. How can I propose a reflection about an ethics in criticism (an ethics requires a community) from these individualistic grounds? But the risk of a limited personalism, I think, is a risk worth running—at least the movement of a few more degrees in self-consciousness—in order to maintain an edge of surprise in the predictable margins of organized resistances.[10]

If we further entertain the notion that the recognition of zones and boundaries is not necessarily the gesture of a personal territorialism— a nationalism of the "I"—but rather the very condition of exchange with another limited other, the contract of this writing and reading then can be seen as the chance for a vividly renegotiated sociality.

This is easier said than done. On the occasions I record here, I have been scheduled explicitly or implicitly as the "feminist" speaker. There is nothing surprising in this (after all, I am a feminist critic and grateful to be invited altogether) or wrong. I think it's a good thing that feminists get asked to speak (even if they are meant only to be the gender-token in the round up of the usual theory suspects). But what chance does any "I" have of undercutting its customary self-representation in the face of the expectations accompanying an "as a": the burden of "speaking for"? When I first gave "Philoctetes' Sister: Feminist Literary Criticism and the New Misogyny," I explained that it was part of this book then called "The Occasional Feminist" (my hope for some time off from my "as a" performances). In the question period, an assistant professor speaking "as a feminist" critic, prefaced her remarks—about the fate of feminist critics in departmental demographics: isn't one enough?—by saying that I wasn't an occasional feminist but an established feminist (one of the ones, presumably, who are enough). For her, there was no way I could make the very distinction I needed to answer her question—from her side: that her department had to be led to see that there were important differences among feminists and that therefore one couldn't possibly be enough (is one Shakespearean enough?). To be sure, she wasn't entirely wrong to refuse my claims for particularities within feminism: hadn't I just given a paper in which I myself say that I am standing in feminism's place and receive, as a "convenient metonymy," the attacks directed at it? Can I have it both ways? That is the project of this book: to make room for both the identification and the difference. Can this be done?

There's a danger in being born with a decade, or almost. One tends to conflate (solipsistically) things that might not have anything to do with each other. The 1970s were my thirties; the 1980s my forties. I've become middle-aged along with the coming of age (the so-called institutionalization) of feminist criticism. Having gotten through the eighties (and Reagan) in feminism, *with* feminism, however, I confess to feeling a good deal more sanguine about feminism than about me: after all, this wave of the movement—as well, of course, as the new generations moving within it—is a lot younger than I am and better prepared to work for change.

I will have finished writing this book on leave in Paris in the course of an academic calendar measured not by seminars but by weekly sessions of physical therapy. I can't help noticing that the city I used to associate nostalgically with the sixties of my youth and their scenarios of seduction has become for me a scene of reeducation—recovering the use of my right arm. I have spent a great deal of time coping with what in English is familiarly called "frozen shoulder" by swimming laps (slowly) in the municipal pool across the street. As I come to the end of this reflection, I am tempted by my therapist's discourse. She can see that I'm getting bored with the sessions of pain, and wondering whether if we stopped, my shoulder wouldn't unblock all by itself. She regularly explains, as if to a hopelessly recalcitrant pupil, that "the last degrees are the hardest." I have always liked maxims and find her youthful sententiousness amusing. Since she has seen the movie of *Les Liaisons dangereuses* (and has told me she's reading the novel), I return, as a former critic of Laclos's libertine plot, with one of its guiding principles: "the first step is the hardest" (my sententiousness).

Still, I'm grateful to have added the "last degrees" to my repertoire, since it is precisely the difficulty of those negotiations with limits that I've been trying to embody in the writing of this book. The gamble involves repersonalizing my work *in* feminism in order to mark for myself the distinction between (which is not the same thing as a disaffection from) me and feminism, me and its occasions—even at the cost of some embarrassment—in order, as we enter the nineties, to inaugurate the writing of my fifties.

Paris, 1990

NOTES

The title of this book takes as its intertexts Elizabeth W. Bruss's *Autobiographical Acts* and Albert E. Stone's *Autobiographical Occasions and Original Acts*.

I borrow the term "feminist confession" from Rita Felski's *Beyond Feminist Aesthetics*.

1. A mailing to the membership in November 1989 both expressed concern "about incidents of antifeminist harassment," qualified by the Commission as a "backlash against feminism" and solicited "personal statements" in order to pursue the inquiry.

2. As in the predictably witless commentary on the 1989 MLA convention in the *New Republic* entitled, "Jargonaut," January 29, 1990.

3. I don't mean the stylistic adjustments from an oral talk to a written essay, but the evacuation of the event itself. An example of an essay strikingly improved by the reinclusion of the occasional frame is Alice Walker's "*One* Child of One's Own." Reprinted in her own book *In Search of Our Mothers' Gardens* four years after its appearance in Janet Sternberg's *The Writer on Her Work*, Walker's essay names its context—a day honoring Muriel Rukeyser at Sarah Lawrence College, and the author's relation to Rukeyser, a teacher to whom, Walker writes, "the creation of the address I am about to give is especially indebted" (361). Rukeyser's notion of "The Child" provides an important dimension to Walker's analysis of "a"/her child.

4. To be sure, many academics proceed more efficiently and subordinate the occasion to the unfolding process of their work, which results in the chapter read aloud *as* the occasion. And just as many graciously acknowledge the scenes—campuses and

gatherings—in which they have shared their work. The emphasis I want to bring to bear here is on the scenes occasioned by that activity in a collective context.

5. These call for an account of the sort I only adumbrate here. The most famous of such occasions in recent history is probably the "sexuality conference" ("The Scholar and the Feminist," 1982, held at Barnard College) which became text in *Pleasure and Danger*, although the details of what actually happened there were not included in the volume's introduction.

As far as my own work is concerned, I have indicated in the table of contents the occasions formative in the construction of the pieces in question, or crucial to their revisions. I have acknowledged with gratitude in footnotes the other contexts in which I had the opportunity to present my work.

6. Mary Jacobus has written eloquently about the uses of metaphor for feminist theorization in her discussion of Irigaray, George Eliot, and the politics of women's writing in *Reading Woman*. Patricia Yaeger argues in *Honey-Mad Women*, specifically for the uses of metaphor as another form of theorization by privileging them in her readings of women's writing. Yaeger, whose thinking here is close to my own, argues for the advantages of the "workaday" character of metaphor, the fact that it provides "ordinary access to extraordinary thinking that we may not yet have tried." "Thus," she goes on to say, "a new metaphor can prove useful in engendering new forms of speculation." Metaphors "can bring separate spheres of knowledge together, collapsing them into enlightening, encompassing icons" (33).

7. Stephen Heath, to whom I owe this reference, reads Barthes's remarks with great attentiveness and pursues the implications of this position against positions; in "Male Feminism" Heath argues that a new marginalism, while perhaps potentially radicalizing for men, has little to offer women in the way of novelty.

8. This sense of physical detail rejoins Naomi Schor's argument in *Reading in Detail* about the potential aesthetic power of the detail as resistance to violence. On the materiality of discourses and their power to hurt, see Wittig's "The Mark of Gender."

9. Deborah McDowell makes the point sharply in a recent interview with Susan Fraiman in *Critical Texts*: "There's a lot of radical criticism that gets the grammar right, but we have become much too comfortable with radical language and not sufficiently committed to radical action. . . . We're in an era that privileges oppositional criticism, yet this criticism can sometimes be an act of substitution" (25).

10. In *Thinking Through the Body* Jane Gallop writes of her essay on *The Pleasure of the Text*: " 'The Perverse Body' tries to think differently the relation between individualism (perversion) and moralism (political responsibility)" (117). Although she comes to no firm conclusion about how to rethink the relation between the individual and morality, her disambiguation of the contradiction—staged in the introduction to the book as a thinking *through* Barthes and Rich—has been productive for my own reflection.

Acknowledgments

I am grateful to the National Endowment for the Humanities whose generous support gave me the time away from teaching in 1989–90 to complete the writing of this book.

I am also indebted to the patience and criticism of many friends, colleagues, and students, who read and commented generously on all or parts of the ms. at various stages of its progress. I would like to express my appreciation in particular to Rachel Brownstein, Mary Ann Caws, Diana Fuss, Jane Gallop, Carolyn Heilbrun, Marianne Hirsch, Alice Kaplan, Sandra Kemp, Sally O'Driscoll, Naomi Schor, Brenda Silver, Margaret Waller, Susan Winnett, and Patricia Yaeger. I'm especially grateful to Sandy Petrey, who thinks autobiographical criticism is self-indulgent pap, for bearing with it anyway: in person. And to Donald Petrey for fixing my math problem.

Over the last few years I have incurred a large and oustanding debt to Elizabeth Houlding, my assistant on this and other projects: I owe the remains of my sanity to her kindnesses.

William P. Germano won my heart when he decided to do this book with me, and Sally O'Driscoll when she saw me through its final stages. I thank Karen Sullivan for moderating the rigors of production.

Finally, I would finally like to thank the members of three seminars whose interventions have played a role in my thinking not easy to acknowledge directly: the NEH Summer Seminar of 1987 on "Issues in Feminist Criticism," my doctoral seminar on "Feminist Poetics" at the Graduate Center, Spring 1988, and "The Subjects of Feminist Criticism" at the School of Criticism and Theory, Summer 1988. This book returns to them.

Some of the essays in this volume have appeared elsewhere in slightly different form. I gratefully acknowledge permission to reprint from the following original sources:

"Creating Feminist Works." The Women's Center, Barnard College, 1978.

"Mastery, Identity, and the Politics of Work: A Feminist Teacher in the Graduate Classroom." *Feminist Pedagogy: Positions and Points of View*, Women's Research Center Working Papers Series (Madison, Wisconsin) (1981) 3; reprinted in *Gendered Subjects: The Dynamics of Feminist Teaching*, ed. Margo Culley and Catherine Portugues. Boston: Routledge and Kegan Paul, 1985.

"Parables and Politics: Feminist Criticism in 1986." *Paragraph* 8 (October 1986).

"My Father's Penis." Afterword to *Refiguring the Father: New Feminist Readings of Patriarchy*, ed. Patricia Yaeger and Beth Kowaleski-Wallace. Carbondale: Southern Illinois University Press, 1989.

I

Getting Personal:
Autobiography as Cultural Criticism

> There is no theory that is not a fragment, carefully preserved,
> of some autobiography.
>
> —Paul Valéry

What's personal criticism? Personal criticism, as I mean the term in this book, entails an explicitly autobiographical performance within the act of criticism. Indeed, getting personal in criticism typically involves a deliberate move toward self-figuration, although the degree and form of self-disclosure of course vary widely. The examples cited below reflect those differences in style and tone: at one end of the scale, for instance, we might place an academic (degree-zero) anecdote from the authorizing groves of campus life, such as the one that launches Stanley Fish's "Is There a Text in this Class?" (recast by Mary Jacobus in "Is There a Woman in this Text?"); at the other, a fully elaborated critical narrative like Rachel Brownstein's ironic reading-memoir *Becoming a Heroine* or Eve Kosofsky Sedgwick's mixed genre self-portrait in "A Poem Is Being Written."

But are autobiographical and personal criticism the same thing? Mary Ann Caws, who has recently defined personal criticism in *Women of Bloomsbury* as being characterized by "a certain intensity in the lending of oneself" to the act of writing, argues that this "participation in the subject seen and written about" (2) doesn't necessarily require autobiographical self-representation.[1] Autobiographical or personal— the distinction is important but the *effects* of the practices, I think, matter more than the nomenclature—the essays under discussion in

I

Personal criticism ~~and reflexive ethnography~~

this chapter raise crucial questions about the constitution of critical authority and the production of theory, and it is in the context of that reflection that I will be mapping their operations.

Personal criticism continued: there is self-narrative woven into critical argument, like Adrienne Rich's reflection on going to visit Emily Dickinson's house in Amherst, Alice Walker's revision of Woolf through her daughter's eye in "*One* Child of One's Own," and Cora Kaplan's interleaving of political and autobiographical argument in *Sea Changes*; or the insertion of framing or interstitial material—like Jane Gallop's recontextualized self-productions (lovers and outfits) in *Thinking Through the Body*. Personal criticism can take the form of punctuating self-portrayal like Carolyn Heilbrun's account in *Writing a Woman's Life* of inventing Amanda Cross; Barbara Johnson's third-person cameo in "Gender Theory and the Yale School"; the appearance of Stephen Heath's sick mother at the end of "Male Feminism"; Frank Lentricchia's invocation of working-class Italian parents in "Andiamo!" (the coda to his polemic—with photos of the author—against Gilbert and Gubar's "essentialist feminism"); the coda to D.A. Miller's "*Cage aux folles*" about the author's shoulder muscle spasm; and structurally discrete anecdote like Stephen Greenblatt's airline encounter that forms an epilogue to *Renaissance Self-Fashioning*. All function as a kind of internal signature or autographics.[2]

Personal criticism may include self-representation as political representativity, like Barbara Smith's plea, in "Toward a Black Feminist Criticism," for women, as she puts it, like herself—members of the black lesbian community; for women across cultures, like Gloria Anzaldúa's "La Prieta," or Cherríe Moraga's "La Güera"; and Gayatri Spivak's ongoing dialogics between her first-world and third-world incarnations in "French Feminism in an International Frame"—and elsewhere; or for other men, like Joseph Boone's "Of Me(n) and Feminism." Personal criticism has engendered experiments in form like Rachel Blau DuPlessis's "For the Etruscans," Patricia Williams's montage of personal and legal anecdote, "On Being the Object of Property," Ann Snitow's counterpoint of argument and diary in "A Gender Diary," or Susan J. Leonardi's "Recipes for Reading." This has also meant the head-on attempt to articulate the personal and the theoretical together, like Carolyn Steedman's *Landscape for a Good Woman* that elaborates a model of working-class female development through maternal biography; Alice Kaplan's *Confessions of a Francophile*, an intellectual autobiography of her relation to "Frenchness"; the narrative of self-authorization on both sides of the maternal divide which is the introduction to Marianne Hirsch's *The Mother/Daughter Plot*; and finally collections of cultural criticism articulated through personal narrative like Joan Nestle's *A Restricted Country*, Mab Segrest's *My Mama's Dead Squirrel*, Audre Lorde's *Sister Outsider*, June Jordan's *Civil Wars*, Bell Hooks's *Talking Back*; and edited volumes like *This Bridge Called My Back*, *Between Women*, or *Gendered Subjects*. The list is far from complete.[3]

Why personal criticism now? Is it another form of "Anti-Theory"? Is it a new stage of theory? Is it gendered? Only for women and gay men? Is it bourgeois? postmodern? A product of Late Capitalism? Reaganomics? Post-feminism? It might be possible, and the reflexes of my structuralist training make me contemplate the project, to construct a typology, a poetics of the "egodocuments"[4] that constitute personal criticism: confessional, locational, academic, political, narrative, anecdotal, biographematic, etc. But is it really a good idea?[5] One of the resistances already mounted against personal criticism is the specter of recuperation: what if what seems new and provocative just turned out to be an academic fashion, another "congealed" genre, as a skeptical colleague put it to me?[6] What if everyone started doing it? I will return to these questions later in the essay. I want to begin instead by noting quickly that I am dealing with material largely produced in the United States in the decades of the 1980s—there are some examples from the late 1970s. (In England it was suggested to me that being "personal" was in fact being American!) *cultural identity*

Our point of entry into this new cultural domain will be a single, or rather a paired example: an essay and a reply to it, in order to have a closer look at what personal criticism seems to be trying to do and what might be at stake in the process. In a recent collection of essays called *Gender and Theory: Dialogues on Feminist Criticism* (1989),

Getting Personal

Jane Tompkins's "Me and My Shadow" (1987) is reprinted along with a reply to it by Gerald MacLean entitled "Citing the Subject." Both are placed in an editorial section called "The Body Writing/Writing the Body," which opens with a quotation from Adrienne Rich (cited by MacLean), that "every mind resides in a body." Personal criticism, as we will see, is often located in a specified body (or voice) marked by gender, color, and national origin: a little like a passport.

I have chosen the Tompkins essay because it self-consciously sets out to embody the claims of personal writing; it is a manifesto, and as such its prose is marked by the rhetorical traits that characterize polemical writing. I was electrified by this piece when it first appeared, despite, or perhaps because of the theoretical difficulties it presents. It seemed to me that its will to be personal was surprising, even in the critical context of a feminism that historically has included and valorized testimonial writing. It is an effort that has inspired mixed reactions, but if anything, the criticism against it (notably MacLean's; his view as the editor, Linda Kauffman, puts it approvingly that Tompkins's "argument reinscribes bourgeois feminism and bourgeois individualism—the very idealist and essentializing strains which so many theorists have tried to dismantle" [119]) makes me want to defend it—if only for the predictability of the critique and of the language it is cast in, even though, as I have said, the essay poses problems; and even though MacLean often identifies them.

"Me and My Shadow" doesn't really need me as public defender. In its reprinted and expanded form, moreover, the essay itself begins with a rejoinder to the accusations the argument has already received from its previous incarnation (as a response to Ellen Messer-Davidow's "The Philosophical Bases of Feminist Literary Criticism," which is also included in the volume):

> Believing that my reply, *which turns its back on theory,* constituted a return to the "rhetoric of presence," to an "earlier, naive, untheoretical feminism," someone, whom I'll call the unfriendly reader, complained that I was making the "old patriarchal gesture of representation" whose effect had been to marginalize women, thus "reinforcing the very stereo-

4

types women and minorities have fought so hard to overcome" (121; emphasis added).

My chief difference with Tompkins's position here is contained in the phrase "which turns its back on theory." What I want to argue— maybe for Tompkins, maybe against her—is that to want to produce and read another kind of writing—a writing from what she will call in this essay, another *voice*, is not necessarily to turn one's back on theory. In my view the case *for* personal writing entails the reclaiming of theory: turning theory back on itself. I will pick up on this issue again, but for now I want to follow out the turns of Tompkins's conviction that to perform this new writing (which is also a reading) requires the rejection of theory because theory exacts as its price the repression of feelings: and the price is too high.

Do you have to turn your back on theory in order to speak with a non-academic voice? "Me and My Shadow" is a meditation on voice. It takes as its subject the epistemological suppositions that according to Messer-Davidow shape feminist work, and moves on to consider the implications for critical writing of the dominant models of access to knowledge. In particular, it focuses on the effects of the splitting off of "private life" and the "merely personal" from conventional academic discourse (122). The essay begins by staging and questioning the "public-private dichotomy, which is to say, the public-private *hierarchy* that is a founding condition," Tompkins argues, "of female oppression. I say to hell with it. The reason I feel embarrassed at my own attempts to speak personally in a professional context is that I have been conditioned to feel that way. That's all there is to it" (123).

Being embarrassed. And then being angry about feeling embarrassed. When you write in a personal voice "in a professional context" about what is embarrassing, who is embarrassed? The writer or the reader? Let me give you the two passages that unfriendly readers can't seem to get past (the second is a reprise of the first).

Most of all, I don't know how to enter the debate [over epistemology] without leaving everything else behind—the birds outside my window, my grief over Janice, just myself as a person sitting here in stockinged feet, a little bit chilly because the windows are open, and thinking about going to the bathroom. But not going yet (126).

(This is what I want you to see. A person sitting in stockinged feet looking out of her window—a floor to ceiling rectangle filled with green, with one red leaf. The season poised, sunny and chill, ready to rush down the incline into autumn. But perfect, and still. Not going yet) (128).

Earlier in the essay, Tompkins describes the pleasure she feels "when a writer introduces some personal bit of story into an essay" because she feels that she is "being allowed to enter into a personal relationship with them" (123). When I read the passages I have just quoted, I was, as she will say later about reading Jessica Benjamin, "hooked." I loved it. But not so much because I felt I had entered a personal relationship with the author—a person in fact I know—but because this inscription of physical detail, this "bit of story" produced for me the portrait of a writer—like me: and in that sense, "just myself as a person." It seemed to me that these passages invoke that moment in writing when everything comes together in a fraction of poise; that fragile moment the writing in turn attempts to capture; and that going to the bathroom, precisely, will end. (If Tompkins were Gallop, the pressure to go would have turned to masturbation; if Tompkins were Barthes, she would have named this with a trope; and by saying that, I'm moving her off the insistence on the signifiers of her phrase that I have identified— "myself as a person"—because it's making me uncomfortable: as a person.)

When I taught this essay (in its 1987 version) for the first time in a seminar called "The Subjects of Feminist Criticism" at the School of Criticism and Theory (1988), I learned something about the effects of embarrassment. Most of the students, especially the women, like the "unfriendly reader" who figures in the new prologue, were unhappy— uncomfortable might be a better word—with the piece; they felt confused and put off by the author's disparagement of the very positions of academic authority they were struggling hard to mime, if not acquire; many of the third-world women—several of whom were not, according to their own declarations, feminist—were made quite angry by the essay's assertions about women and their feelings. Wasn't this what men always thought women were like? How can women get power from this? (Tompkins confesses at the beginning of her essay that this was the way *she* felt about feminist criticism when it first appeared in print.) It's self-indulgent. We don't want to know if she has to go to the bathroom. . . . Men go to the bathroom, too. If a man wrote about going to the bathroom, etc. (Like MacLean, some of the men announced they would like to have heard more about the husband, not named here, but knowable: Stanley Fish.)

I know I was not successful in countering their objections. I know because I'm not sure I can answer them now. I had included the piece in a section of the course called "Whose Theory?" in which we also read Irigaray's "Any Theory of the 'Subject' Has Always Been Appropriated by the 'Masculine,'" Cixous's "The Laugh of the Medusa," Barbara Christian's "The Race for Theory" (included with a reply by Michael Awkward in *Gender and Theory*), and Gloria Anzaldúa's "A Letter to Third World Women Writers," all of which also either mark the body's presence, or personalize it; speak autobiographically or representatively: *for* women, *for* emotion; for putting all that into writing and into the world; against a language of abstraction; against male theories that constitute woman in lack, invisibility, silence. But whatever problems those essays posed—most of which boil down to the ultimate cause of critical dismissal: the charge of essentialism—there was something about "Me and My Shadow" that wouldn't go away.

Is it about going to the bathroom? Or is it about the conditions of critical authority? Or are they the same question? Can what Barthes in *Criticism and Truth* (1966) called the new "critical plausibility" sustain the inclusion of the bathroom? For students, perhaps, Tompkins's announcement of thinking about *going* reactivates one's childhood disbelief that teachers *went* at all. Does the mere mention of the bathroom undermine what Tompkins describes as the "authority effect" in critical writing, "an 'authoritative' language [that] speaks as though the other person weren't there" (129), or does the sense of violation caused by the irruption of the private into the public dominion of academic discourse depend on the perception of authority?[7] To the extent that as academics we worry about our own ability to produce the authority effect, we're not sure we want ourselves going to the bathroom in public—especially as women and feminists—our credibility is low enough as it is. If the figures of personal criticism, like autobiography, embody the writing fiction that another person is there, is this "reading contract" strengthened or weakened by talking about "going" or "not going"?[8]

Critical plausibility like critical pleasure is also a politics. In an age of literary studies where students as well as teachers often spend more time reading critics than authors, when according to a disgruntled old guard, theory has come to replace literature, perhaps the time has come to think about what happens when we read critical writing.

Let me place here an

"Intermezzo: On Roland Barthes"
1. by Jane Gallop
2. by Barbara Christian

1. At the end of *Criticism and Truth*, which is, among other things, a defense of the new criticism he played so important a role in founding, Barthes collapses the distinction between critic and reader, reader and writer he will work so hard to put in place in his famous essay, "The Death of the Author" (published two years later in 1968).

> To read is to desire the work, to want to be the work. . . . To go from reading to criticism is to change desires, it is no longer to desire the work but to desire one's own language. But by that very process it is to send the work back to the desire to write from which it arose. And so discourse circulates around the book: *reading, writing* (93–94).

Being in love with writing, with language, with one's own movement into writing.

Although nothing could be more dangerous in these matters than a bald narrative of causality, a good deal of literary criticism of the late seventies and early eighties in the United States, I want to suggest, can be seen as an effect of this Barthesian circularity connecting the production of critical writing to the love of reading. The foregrounding of this desire for language, in language, as pleasure, produced a crack in academic protocols. As Jane Gallop, a writer with an acute sense of the tensions that underpin critical tact, puts it in *Thinking Through the Body*, explaining the impact of Barthes's work on her own: "When I was a graduate student [in the early seventies] Barthes was the leading literary critic-theorist in French studies. He had already passed out of his scientific stance (structuralism) into something that seemed softer, more subjective, more bodily. The Barthes of the seventies," Gallop continues, "authorized my own push out of objective, scholarly discourse into something more embodied" (11). Despite his critical politics, which, we recall, loathed both the figure of the author as the literary equivalent of the already unappetizing "human person" ("Death," 143) and that of the Critic who sustained the reign of authorial privilege through explication, by bringing into critical language through the tropes of desire, "something . . . softer, more subjective, more bodily," Barthes's writing has—willy-nilly—authorized a variety of forms of critical self-fabrication.[9] Despite his polemic against the "person," and celebration of the empty "subject" of language ("Death," 145), Barthes modeled the possibility of personal criticism through his own extremely sophisticated manipulation of theoretical discourse, which not only made visible the traces of a writing body, but imposed the manners of a strongly biographized—biographemized—rhetorical *personality.*

What gives a reader and a critic pleasure in reading other writers and critics? What produces a kinship of desire to write?

2. In the introduction to a collection of essays on black women writers, Barbara Christian stages a dialogue between her ten-year-old daughter Najuma and herself, while she tries to "work" and withstand her daughter's interruptions. The introduction is called "Black Feminist Process: In the Midst of . . . " and as Christian explains in a later essay, "But What Do We Think We're Doing Anyway," it self-consciously embodies the need for a black feminist criticism to "personalize the staid language associated with the critic . . . and forms that many readers found intimidating and boring" (69). To her daughter's skepti-

9

Selfconscious criticism is alive and well —Virginia Woolf

Isit at my desk and I
write, my book scattered
at my feet fall like the
dried
leaves
scattered
by
Sybil

cal view of her mother's reading as work and her demand to know *why* she is reading, Christian calls up for the reader Foucault's "Fantasia of the Library" and a feminist revision of it that imagines replacing Foucault's male European reader with a woman reader, whom Christian then displaces in turn by thinking that her "black sisters *and* brothers would not even have gotten in the library, or [if they did] they'd be dusting the books" "like the parlour maid in *Jane Eyre*" (ix). Christian thinks aloud, so to speak, about what reading means to her, and in the process, moves from Foucault to Barthes, via her recollected schoolgirl readings of Nancy Drew and her recent reading of Alice Walker:

> When I read something that engages me, my reaction is visceral: I sweat, get excited, exalted or irritated, scribble on the edges of the paper, talk aloud to the unseen writer or to myself. Like the Ancient Mariner, I waylay every person in my path, "Have you read this? What about this, this, or this?" This reaction is no news to my daughter. She and her friends get that way about Michael Jackson, TV shows, stickers, possibly even Judy Blume. But that response, of course, is not so much the accepted critical mode, despite Barthes's *plaisir*. It's too suspect, too subjective, not grounded in reality (xi).

Najuma is persistent. She wants to know why her mother needs to write down what she thinks and feels about a book, why not just pick up the phone and call Alice [Walker], "why not just tell Alice about her book?" "Writing, she knows," Christian remarks, "is even more private than reading, which separates her from me and has many times landed her in bed before she wanted to go. I smile. Barthes's comment, 'Writing is precisely that which exceeds speech,' comes to mind. I pause" (xiii). Christian doesn't succeed in persuading her daughter of the virtues of reading and writing: "It sounds to me like too much work," Najuma concludes, "why don't you get involved with the airlines, so we can travel free."

Here, as in her essay "The Race for Theory," Christian condemns the "metaphysical language" in which a hegemonic elite argues that "philosophers are the ones who write literature, that authors are dead, irrelevant, mere vessels through which their narratives ooze, that they do not work nor have they the faintest idea what they are doing; rather, they produce texts as disembodied as the angels" (230), and like Tompkins, what interests her, what seems alive (on the side of her daughter, and not the angels) is *process*.[10]

> Can one theorize effectively about an evolving process? Are the labels informative or primarily a way of nipping the question in the bud? What are the philosophical assumptions behind my praxis? I think how the articulation of a theory is a gathering place, sometimes a point of rest as the process rushes on, insisting that you follow. I can see myself trying to explain those tiers of books to my daughter as her little foot taps the floor (xi).

Both Christian and Tompkins see theory as something that like the scene of Foucault's library weighs down the writer for whom the tiers of books hold the wrong questions, or ask them in the wrong language, what Tompkins calls in her essay, following Ursula LeGuin, "the screen of forced language" of "the father tongue" (127). The books make no room for the personal and banish feeling. For Tompkins and Christian, the mind/body, theory/process, post-structuralism/feminism splits seem too unequal and too powerful for negotiation; for Gallop, however, if the splits require demystification, the one doesn't prevent her from access to the other: "In collecting my essays for this retrospective volume," she writes, "I found myself adding autobiographical bits, not only, I hope, because I tend toward exhibitionism but, more important, because at times I think through autobiography: that is to say, the chain of associations that I am pursuing in my reading passes through things that happened to me" (4). For Gallop this "passage between theory and life story is paved by . . . American feminism and French post-structuralism" (5); by the writing of Adrienne Rich and Roland Barthes.

End of "Intermezzo"

In one of the segments of "Me and My Shadow" added to the original version, the author scans the books on her shelf, picking up and dipping into Guattari, Bloom, Foucault, and as a point of contrast, an essay by Jessica Benjamin on erotic domination (collected in the anthology *The Powers of Desire*). Tompkins tries to determine why these writers—but I will just take up her instance of Foucault (a writer, of whom she says, she has been "an extravagant admirer" [133])—fail now to engage her as a reader, and why Benjamin turns her on, gets her juices flowing. She resists his use of "we"— "the convention in which the author establishes common ground with his reader by using the first-person plural . . . . It is chummy this 'we.' It feels good, for a little while, until it starts to feel coercive, until 'we' are subscribing to things that 'I' don't believe. There is no specific reference to the author's self, no attempt to specify himself" (132–33).

To her discomfort with Foucault's generalizations about Victorian sexuality, Tompkins contrasts her excitement as a reader at Benjamin's account of erotic domination: "I am completely hooked, I am going to read this essay from beginning to end and proceed to do so. In fact . . . I find myself putting it down and straying from it because the subject is *so* close to home . . . " (133–34). But then, she has a problem with the logic of her own argument: "There is no personal reference here. The author deals, like Foucault, in generalities . . . Why am I not turned off by this as I was in Foucault's case?" (134) Why do Benjamin's abstractions seem concrete and Guattari's alienating (131)? Subject matter? Or writing subject?[11] Tompkins concludes that there is no way to determine what turns whom on: for Guattari it's the "machine," Bloom, the Sublime: "What is personal," she has to concede tautologically, "is completely a function of what is perceived as personal" (134).

Now that's fine as a democratic principle, exemplary of the sixties some of us remember. But that is not where Tompkins is moving the argument; she is moving it toward a claim for sexual difference.

> And what is perceived as personal by men, or rather, what is gripping, significant, "juicy," is different from what is felt to be that way by women. For what we are really talking about is not the personal as such, what we are talking about is what is important, answers one's needs, strikes one as immediately *interesting*. For women, the personal is such a category (134).

To write in 1989—or even in 1987—that men and women have radically, essentially different apprehensions of what is personal is to raise the critical hackles of a whole variety of "unfriendly readers": what interests women is the personal[12]; this is probably worse than going—or not going to the bathroom—which as one of my students complained, isn't even personal. But I'm going to bracket the specter of a monolithic female-culture position in order to recast the assertion as a question: if what seems important (*"interesting"*) to women is personal, what seems important and interesting to men? Or in terms of critical politics—which does and doesn't always match with gender—what over the last three decades has seemed interesting generally? This is a question Tompkins doesn't answer in her essay directly. She offers instead the following narrative of the trajectory that the category of the person in literary criticism has taken since the late 1950s:

> In literary criticism, we have moved from the New Criticism, which was anti-personal and declared the personal off-limits at every turn—the intentional fallacy, the affective fallacy—to structuralism, which does away with the self altogether—at least as something unique and important to consider—to deconstruction, which subsumes everything in language and makes the self non-selfconsistent, ungraspable, a floating signifier, and finally to new historicism which re-institutes the discourse of the object—"In the seventeenth century"—with occasional side glances at how the author's "situatedness" affects his writing.

> The female subject *par excellence,* which is her self and her experiences, has once more been elided by literary criticism.

> The question is, why did this happen? One might have imagined a different outcome. The 1960s paves the way for a new personalism in literary discourse by opening literary discussion up to politics, to psychology, to the "reader," to the effects of style. What happened to deflect criticism into the impersonal labyrinths of "language," "discourse," "system," "network," and now, with Guattari, "machine"? (135)

In its characterizations of these critical movements, Tompkins's chronology is largely accurate. MacLean, however, criticizes the "progress form" of her account, and its omissions: "What really astonishes me about your defeatist narrative is how it reinscribes the phallic narrative of progress for the sake of a reactionary, anti-feminist argument that is, in any case, true only to the extent that it ignores important work by feminist critics" (145). I can only assume here that in her

narrative, Tompkins is not ignoring "important work by feminist critics"—forgetting, notably, her own book *Sensational Designs* and her
teaching—but rather is choosing to outline the great march of critical
modes, which effectively have tended to favor the authority of the
impersonal: she is, after all, making a point about dominant criticism.
But since Tompkins in fact doesn't talk specifically about feminist
theory and its epistemological (that word again) relation to the personal, I want to invoke it briefly. Specifically, I think we need to
understand the highly charged ways in which the personal and impersonal modes of critical discourse both coexist and struggle against each
other within feminism, and between feminism and dominant criticisms.

Feminist theory has always built out from the personal: the witnessing "I" of subjective experience. The notion of the "authority of
experience" founded a central current in feminist theory in the 1970s
and continues—dismantled and renovated—to shape a variety of personal and less personal discourses at an oppositional angle to dominant
critical positionings. But despite that foundational construction, most
academic women in the 1970s did not articulate that as a "new personalism" in their writing. In literary studies, the works of pioneering
feminist literary scholars—like Kate Millett, Ellen Moers, Sandra Gilbert and Susan Gubar, Elaine Showalter, Annette Kolodny, and Judith
Fetterley—were clearly fueled by a profound understanding of the
consequences of taking the personal as a category of thought and
gender as a category of analysis. But as academic feminists—and I'm
talking here of white mainstream feminism—they on the whole wrote
like everyone else who belongs to the third sex of "Ph.D.'s" Carolyn
Heilbrun has added to the categories of male and female readers ("Millett's *Sexual Politics*," 39).[13] This self-conscious depersonalization was
increased in the mid-eighties with a certain level of institutionalization,
by which I mean the construction and recognition of feminist theory
as a body of knowledge, as well as by the "theory" frenzy that affected
most academic writing—at least on the level of the signifier. At the
same time, however, the experiments in autobiographical or personal
criticism that I have been describing were also going on and constituted

a contrapuntal effect, breaking into the monolithic and monologizing authorized discourse.

The kind of writing that was polemical, overtly political, often anecdotal, and shaped by the intensity of personal voice that Tompkins calls for in this essay tended to occur in another literary genre, occasional writing: writing for sessions at the MLA sponsored by the Commission on the Status of Women, at Women's Studies conferences, in feminist anthologies, newsletters etc. Academic women wanting jobs and tenure (and most of us did) conformed to the "critical plausibility" of their scene and cohort which required an objective style.

In particular, feminist teaching tended to produce a great deal of personal testimony. In "Deconstruction, Feminism, and Pedagogy" (written in 1985, published in 1987) for instance, Barbara Johnson, setting de Manian deconstruction (referring specifically to "The Resistance to Theory," an essay from 1982) in relation to a volume on feminist pedagogy called *Gendered Subjects* (1985), evaluates the effects of the personal as a critical intervention:

> The title *Gendered Subjects* . . . indicates a move to reverse the impersonal-
> ization that de Man radicalizes and to reintroduce the personal, or at least
> the positional, as a way of disseminating authority and decomposing the
> false universality of patriarchally institutionalized meanings. Not only
> has personal experience tended to be excluded from the discourse of
> knowledge, but the realm of the personal itself has been coded as female
> and devalued for that reason. In opposition, therefore, many of the essays
> of the volume consciously assume a first-person autobiographical stance
> toward the question of pedagogical theory (43–44).

If self-resistance is "a form of resistance to the very notion of a self," and in de Man's words, "the only teaching worthy of the name is *scholarly, not personal*" (43; emphasis added), it's not immediately clear what the two pedagogies can be doing together. But because Barbara Johnson thinks like Barbara Johnson, she cannot leave the construction in place and goes on to ask whether "the depersonalization of deconstruction and the repersonalization of feminism" aren't "in reality haunted by the ghost of the other" (44). "Against" the grain of feminism, Johnson worries that "the moment one assumes one knows what female experience is, one runs the risk of creating another reductive appropriation—an appropriation that consists in the reduction of experience *as* self-resistance" (46). Of the paradox that "it was precisely [de Man's] way of denying personal authority that engendered the unique power of his personal authority" (45), Johnson wonders aloud, pressing on what is a crucial question about person, authority, and critical authorship:

> why de Man's discourse of self-resistance and uncertainty has achieved such authority and visibility, while the self-resistance and uncertainty of *women* has been part of what has insured their lack of authority and their invisibility. It would seem that one has to be positioned in the place of power in order for one's self-resistance to be valued. Self-resistance, indeed, may be one of the few viable postures remaining for the white male establishment (45).

Johnson does not go on to recommend that women seek to overcome self-resistance through the validation of "experience" because she sees the personal narratives meant to revalidate female experience as tending toward the abstraction of a re-depersonalized "we women": do all women share a single personal narrative? In the passage from one feminist teacher's (Susan Stanford Friedman's) experience in the classroom to a generalization about conditions "we all face," Johnson reads the seductions of abstraction and the twin dangers of depersonalization and essentialism. This is fair to a point, but misses, I think, both the historicity of that move from "I" to "we"—the sense of intellectual experiment and innovative practice of the late seventies in the United States, and the feeling of excitement the idea of community negotiates: the possibility that there might be enough feminist teachers out there to collaborate—as opposed to lonely brave souls in hostile environments, and the rhetorical buoyancy engendered by that possibility.

At this juncture in my own account I am in fact wanting to argue two things: that the personal and the positional (to take up Johnson's terms) are both the same and different. Or, that what feminist theory is about is the effort to analyze that relation. Which brings us back to the business at hand: Tompkins on Messer-Davidow, MacLean on

Tompkins. What is at stake in these exchanges is precisely the tension between personal and positional modes of authority in writing and in the classroom that Johnson looks at in her examples.

"How can we speak personally to one another and yet not be self-centered?" (129), Tompkins asks; rephrased by MacLean, the question drops the matter of the addressee (146), which is to say, the other party in the self-fiction of the personal writer. And that is perhaps the biggest problem of MacLean's response: to whom is it written? for whom is it written? Who does he imagine the audience of this self-representation to be? Feminist critics? Men, like him, ostensibly wanting to "be" in feminism (or at least hang out in the neighborhood)? To some extent of course, the problem is not only his. It is a problem of genre: to whom does one answer in a published reply? Tompkins writes: "My response to this essay is not a response to something Ellen Messer-Davidow has written; it is a response to something within myself. As I reread the opening pages I feel myself being squeezed into a strait-jacket; I wriggle, I will not go in" (128). Tompkins produces both the voice of the straitjacket: a straight reply, and the other voice: "Just me and my shadow, walkin' down the avenue" (128). MacLean tries to reply to Tompkins's other voice by opening his reply in the form of a letter in which he explains what each of them is doing[14]: "Dear Jane, This is not, then, a journal. This is a response to your response to Ellen Messer-Davidow's essay . . . . Your argument for the return of the authorial body . . . is an exploration of the psychoanalytical self inhab-iting the *persona* of a professional intellectual . . . . I am interested in the political limits and implications of your call for the return of the person" (142–43). "Dear Gerald," I feel like writing back. "Try a letter *to a person.*"

MacLean cannot seem to write without condescending to women, and he allows himself the maddening self-indulgence of doing it and calling himself on it: "So here I am, doing what I was trained to do, telling 'women' what to do, how to think and behave" (148). The challenge, therefore, for me in writing about this in my turn is not simply to condescend *as a feminist* to him *as a man*: in part, because that is the path of least resistance—the cross-gender sniping of heterosexual

17

couples this paired reply structure sets up[15]; in part because it perpetu-
ates the very relations with women and feminists he describes in his
essay: the eternal circle of men and feminism and on and on. And yet
how to read this text without sounding like the feminist police?[16]

The essay by Adrienne Rich from which MacLean quotes in his
reply to Tompkins is called "Taking Women Students Seriously." First
published in 1979, it is reprinted in *Gendered Subjects*. Rich's reminder
that "every mind resides in a body" leads to MacLean's first stab at
"personal criticism" in the essay. But to do so he begins by identifying
himself as a "as a"—"as a white, heterosexual, first-world male writing
about feminism"—and by recasting Tompkins's project via Marx and
Derrida (which requires three footnotes, two by Marx): "What, I
believe, Tompkins has in mind is not so much the return of the 'person'
behind the newly enfranchised 'voice' of the 'woman'—though she
might well be read this way—but the displacement of the authority of
the text by the supplement of the writer" (142). Having recast the very
terms of Tompkins's repertory—person, voice, woman (in his words,
"problematizing [her] recuperation of authorial presence" [142]),
MacLean relocates himself under the feminist authority of Alice Jardine
and Gayatri Spivak. To Jardine's challenge to men to "talk their bodies" (146) MacLean responds with discussions of his relations with his
students, his mother, and his wife. I've chosen to focus here primarily
on MacLean's self-portrait as a teacher since feminist pedagogy is one
of the central concerns of this book:

> There are difficulties in my trying to teach women students from a "femi-
> nist" stance. I don't think anyone has begun to examine fully the range
> of erotic interactions that go on between students and teachers. In class I
> flirt, consciously and consistently. But I play for laughs and flirt with the
> men too. I talk about sex a good deal, distinguish it from sexuality and
> gender, demonstrate how lifeless the canonical works we must read would
> be without this discourse of sex, and introduce marginal texts which
> problematize sexual relationships. Teaching in North America, my privi-
> leged (English) accent helps a great deal: I can parrot Monty Python
> voices. My body helps too: over six feet long and skinny, limp-wristed
> but capable of dashing gestures. Being a man, with this voice and this

body, it is easy to play between the farcical and serious modes. Yet like all teachers, I can never fully know just what effect(s) I have (149).

The title of the Rich essay MacLean referred to, we recall, is "Taking Women Students Seriously." Part of what goes wrong here for me is his claim that exploiting the erotic potential of the classroom by flirting with the women students while talking (suavely) about sex makes progress in that direction. What could take women less seriously than repositioning them (us) as the audience of the most conventional heterosexuality on display; women who, as Rich notes—and the situation has in no way improved—on college campuses live in a climate of authorized sexual harassment. (That he flirts with the men *too* doesn't change the basic assumptions of the model.) The problem here, I think, is that MacLean's personal can't escape the positional: the idiosyncratic biographemes of accent and size leave intact the structural features of sexual politics in the classroom. He identifies with his role (he plays with putting it on, can he take it off?), still canonically male—despite the so-called feminization of the profession: the professor of desire.

But what's personal? Who decides? What's more personal: Tompkins looking out the window in her stockinged feet—and not going to the bathroom; MacLean flirting in the classroom; Christian talking to her daughter; Gallop invoking her debt to Roland Barthes; Stephen Heath talking about his relation to feminism? Is it personal only if it's embarrassing? If not, is it just a rhetorical ploy? Do I wind up saying that "bad" politics aren't personal? Or am I saying, if I like it, it's personal, it caresses me; otherwise, it's just positional, it aggresses me. Am I being politically correct again? Maybe personal criticism is for women only. Or do women seem better at it because they've been awash in the personal for so long? Is it political? Is it theoretical? What's the point of personal criticism? Why now?

Most of these questions, which I bracketed at the start, are going to get short shrift again since I'm writing this essay to illuminate an unfolding phenomenon and I don't want to foreclose its effects. But a few remarks are in order. It seems to me that the efflorescence of personal criticism in the United States in the eighties—like the study of autobiography—has in part to do with the gradual, and perhaps inevitable waning of enthusiasm for a mode of Theory, whose authority—however variously—depended finally on the theoretical evacuation of the very social subjects producing it (the upset and uproar surrounding the revelations about Paul de Man's biography figure, I think, both the limits and the costs of this fiction). It might also be fruitful to understand this aspect of what Laura Kipnis has described as the "hypervisibility" of the "ideological category of the subject" (158) as having to do with the emergence of global movements of liberation; the pressure in this post-colonial moment for more complex modulations of agency, capable of articulating the internal contradictions of subjectivity under "late capitalism."[17] This latter configuration has given rise paradoxically both to "identity politics"—the claims arising from a repertoire of often conflicting social inscriptions—and its repudiation (dunned internally by the antiessentialist discourses and externally exploded by geopolitical catastrophes).

But if "identity politics" has challenged bourgeois self-representation—with all its unself-conscious exclusions—speaking "as a" has emerged as an equally problematic *representativity*. Indeed, one of the reasons for the current proliferation of autobiographical criticism may well be the effect of a crisis over that representativity: an anxiety over speaking *as* and speaking *for*, doubling the postmodern crisis of representation that has been so repetitively diagnosed. Though the reign of the Master Narratives, we are told, has passed, micro-narratives abound, and with them a massive reconsideration of the conditions grounding authorization itself. At the same time, moreover, through a paradox of reversible effects we are now becoming familiar with, the poststructuralist lesson and the postmodern moment have powerfully imprinted on contemporary productions of identity writing.[18]

Let us turn now to the matter of gender and theory, and the degree to which their troubled relations might help us understand what's going on in the cases at hand. To the extent that one of feminism's

principal subjects has been an interrogation of the production of
knowledge as a highly contextual activity, it is not surprising that the
personalization of cultural analysis should emerge out of its zones of
inquiry. This of course does not mean either that only women who are
feminists or that all feminists do personal criticism; rather, that the
material is there as well as a history of praxis. Men's relations to the
personal, on the one hand, and to the theoretical, on the other, have
on the whole remained both so falsely transparent and so dispropor-
tionately weighted to the side of theory that it would be more than
foolish to foreclose the discussion—already bogged down in "men in
feminism"—by yet another set of generalizations. Locally, the problem
with "Citing the Subject," I think, is a function of its author's resistance
to the challenge feminism brings to refiguring subjectivity; this reconsti-
tution necessarily passing through displacements within one's relation
to theory's own requirement of what Stephen Heath, in his essay,
"Male Feminism," calls "self-preserve" (12); and to the self-image cast
in writing by the theorist. This is in fact a double challenge: to recast
the subject's relation to itself and to authority, the authority *in* theory.
Where, then, will authority come from? The person(al)?

When Tompkins concludes the new introduction to her essay by
saying: "I now tend to think that theory itself, at least as it is usually
practiced, may be one of the patriarchal gestures women *and* men
ought to avoid" (122), I want to emphasize not the "theory itself," but
the "at least as it is usually practiced." Despite the fact that—argua-
bly—"*theory*," as Heath, following Irigaray, puts it, "with all its reservations, is today a male move, an argument from men" (12), rather
than handing "theory" over to "them," what we can argue about is
precisely the *practice of theory*, and therefore the question of whether
theory can be personalized and the personal theorized.[19]

If one of the original premises of seventies feminism (emerging out
of sixties slogans) was that "the personal is the political," eighties
feminism has made it possible to see that the personal is also the
theoretical: the personal is part of theory's material. Put another way,
what may distinguish contemporary feminism from other postmodern
thought is the expansion in the definition of cultural material.[20]

21

Getting Personal

Thus, in the last segment of her essay (which follows the narrative of critical movements cited above), Tompkins moves into this complexly mapped area of personal, political, and theoretical zones. She describes the occasion in which she (as a visiting lecturer) met Messer-Davidow (as a participant) at the School of Criticism and Theory. That summer (at some point in the mid-eighties) Messer-Davidow organized a symposium on feminist criticism and theory designed, I assume, to dramatize what its absence on the scene as a subject matter (not to say physical reality) might mean. Tompkins describes that action of leadership as "analysis that is not an end in itself but pressure brought to bear on a situation" and "that should be included in our concept of criticism" (135). Although a good one, this is not a difficult point to argue within feminist theory: the value of intervention, of *practical* criticism, of *collective* self-consciousness. But there is also an important turn here.

Tompkins confesses that it is in fact her own rage about the effacement of women that has been the organizing principle of the essay thus far, as well as the wager that what motivated Messer-Davidow was anger at the exclusions of women from the scenes of theory: "I hate men for the way they treat women, and pretending that women aren't there is one of the ways I hate most" (136). But the turn for me is less the revelation of anger than its trope: she has been talking the whole time, she says, about "something . . . [that] doesn't *show*, as we used to say about the slips we used to wear" (135).

If I were to make an authorial—not to say personal—intervention at this point, it would be to say that this is where I have been wanting to come since the beginning: this is it. It has to do with two things that are not only related to each other, but implicated in each other: showing and anger. I want to talk about the affect and effects of self-display, and the spectacle of gender. Let's go back just for a moment to bring these points together, to MacLean's closing remarks which are directed at psychoanalysis and what he calls the "socio-political structuring of the subject or the political redirection of feminist anger" (153). This, for instance, as part of the explanation for why he personally decided not to go into therapy for striking his wife during an argument [151–52]): "Together with the enormous financial investment that therapy

22

represents, with or without medical insurance, this depoliticizing tendency marks the purely psychoanalytical path to personal rehabilitation as suspect for a feminist practice" (153). On that note, MacLean produces a list of feminist scholars who have taught him "where to direct [his] anger" (153), and to them are addressed his last words: "I confidently insist that I know violence need not be the only inevitable result of anger" (154).

The slip of anger passes through the conventions of gender. MacLean comes up against the literature of domestic violence; Tompkins exposes the rage over female invisibility that is structured by the injunction against exposure: the danger for women of making a spectacle of oneself. "There is a phrase," Mary Russo writes in "Female Grotesques," "that still resonates from childhood. Who says it? The mother's voice—not my own mother's, perhaps, but the voice of an aunt, an older sister, or the mother of a friend. It is a harsh matronizing phrase, and it is directed toward the behavior of other women: 'She' [the other woman] is making a spectacle out of herself" (213).

Let us think again now about the reactions to Tompkins's essay through this anxiety about feminine exposure: "the possessors of large, aging, and dimpled thighs displayed at the public beach, of overly rouged cheeks, of a voice shrill in laughter, or of a sliding bra strap— a loose, dingy bra strap especially—were at once caught out by fate and blameworthy" (213). By going/not going to the bathroom in public, Tompkins crosses the line into the dangerous zones of feminine excess.[21] But this intentional calling attention to herself, the deliberate flipside of the inadvertent display of dingy underwear, while to many unfortunate—a lapse in taste—may not be what unfriendly readers finally find most distressing about the essay. It is, I think, less the slip, than the anger; the slipping of anger into the folds of the argument: this anger is not merely a rhetorical trope: it's not supposed to show, but it does.[22] "She" is making a spectacle of herself. "She," as has often been said of me, is "being emotional."

"Just me and my shadow, walkin' down the avenue." The next line of the song goes, "Me and my shadow, all alone and feeling blue." But is the personal critic necessarily alone, immured in isolation?

I would rather argue that this mode of criticism, far from being turned in on itself in a miserable "privatization of the personal" (MacLean, 148), is on the contrary, to bring back an old-fashioned word: engaged. As Mary Ann Caws puts it: "Personal criticism as I intend it has to do with a willing, knowledgeable, outspoken involvement on the part of the critic with the subject matter, and an invitation extended to the potential reader to participate in the interweaving and construction of the ongoing conversation this criticism can be, even as it remains a text" (2). By the risks of its writing, personal criticism embodies a pact, like the "autobiographical pact" binding writer to reader in the fabulation of self-truth, that what is at stake matters also to others: somewhere in the self-fiction of the personal voice is a belief that the writing is worth the risk.[23] In this sense, by turning its authorial voice into spectacle, personal writing theorizes the stakes of its own performance: a personal materialism. Personal writing opens an inquiry on the cost of writing—critical writing or Theory—and its effects. The embarrassment produced in readers is a sign that it is working. At the same time the embarrassment blows the cover of the impersonal as a masquerade of self-effacement—at least by indirection—and points to the narcissistic fantasy that inheres in the poses of self-sufficiency we identify with Theory; notably, those of abstraction.

In the notes to "A Poem Is Being Written," an autobiographical essay that moves out of the erotic pleasure structured in the tableau of spanking (and the rhythms of poetry), originally conceived for a colloquium called the "Poetics of Anger" (Columbia University, 1985), Eve Kosofsky Sedgwick writes: "Part of the motivation behind my work [on the essay] has been a fantasy that readers or hearers would be variously—in anger, identification, pleasure, envy, 'permission,' exclusion—stimulated to write accounts 'like' this one (whatever that means) of their own, and share those" (137). What Sedgwick records here as the author of a personal spectacle is the desire for a response—beyond the specular. This might take the form, for instance, of more personal criticism—this is the hope, I think, of all published autobiographical writing—but also of gestures, not predetermined, that would bring out other voices from their own shadows.[24]

Autobiography as Cultural Criticism

Is the production of other voices and other scenes all there is to it? To be sure, like all writing, personal criticism is only as good as its practitioners. At its worst, it runs the risk of producing a new effect of exclusion, the very "chumminess" of the unidentified "we" of Foucauldian self-effacing authority that Tompkins set out to displace. Who, for instance, my students wanted to know, was the dead friend, Janice? At its worst, the autobiographical act in criticism can seem to belong to a scene of rhizomatic, networked, privileged selves who get to call each other (and themselves) by their first names in print: an institutionally authorized personalism. But at its best, I would argue, the personal in these texts is at odds with the hierarchies of the positional—working more like a relay *between* positions to create critical fluency. Constituted finally in a social performance, these autobiographical acts may produce a new repertory for an enlivening cultural criticism.

Is there a woman in this text? Mary Jacobus asked of Stanley Fish's "anec-joke." The woman in Jane Tompkins's text is a dead woman, a talented younger colleague who killed herself.[25] The spectacle of personal criticism in "Me and My Shadow," which is also, I think, a rage about this death, is a way of calling attention to the living women who are no less the "subject matters" of feminism.

The song goes on: "It's 5 o'clock, We climb the stairs, We never knock, 'Cause nobody's there."

Is there?

NOTES

I am grateful to Maurice Biriotti for inviting me to speak at the seminar he organized with Nicola Miller at Cambridge University under the title. "What Is an Author?" And to Margaret Whitford and David Shepheard, for bringing me to Queen Mary and Westfield College, London, to speak in the context of a research seminar at the Centre for Modern European Studies, February 1990.

I borrow my epigraph from James Olney, who chose it for the epigraph to his anthology *Autobiography: Essays Theoretical and Critical.*

1. Caws describes personal criticism—hers and that of others—with an emphasis on voice and subjectivity that can include the autobiographical, but is more often a matter of intensity in the critical writing itself. For her, as she explains in "Personal

Criticism: A Matter of Choice"—the first chapter of the book—the crucial element of this act involves the mixing of text and critic, and the marking of that interaction in voice, tone, and attitude. In the summer of 1988, she offered a seminar called "Personal Criticism" at the School of Criticism and Theory and in so doing named a modality that I am relocating here to my own ends as part of a wider set of critical activities that have come to be associated with the phrase. I take the term as an umbrella under which to group a variety of critical performances not necessarily "personal" in Caws's formulation.

Rachel Blau DuPlessis describes a practice that combines both Caws's sense of personal and my own of autobiographical criticism in the acknowledgments to her recent collection of essays, *The Pink Guitar*: essays, she writes, "in which elements of guarded, yet frank autobiography, textual analysis, and revisionary myth-making suddenly fused into a demanding voice, with a mix of ecstatic power over cultural materials and mourning for the place of the female in culture" (viii).

2. Heath describes the reference to his mother as "an emotional location of the piece as legitimation" (30). I think this usefully characterizes the strategies of several of these pieces.

I see as a separate variant the use of the "biographeme" (Barthes's term for those details of taste or inflection that function as metonymic marks—volatile signifiers of a recollected but dispersed biographical subject) restricted to the threshold of a book, or the opening moves of an essay—after which the personal vanishes: Naomi Schor's brief memorialization of her father as goldsmith in *Reading in Detail*; Linda Orr's description of the smell of the books she was working on in *Headless Histories*; Charles Bernheimer's invocation of his father in *Flaubert and Kafka*; Susan Suleiman's self-identification as a mother in "Writing Motherhood"; Elaine Showalter's self-fiction as an auburn-haired feminist critic in "Toward a Feminist Poetics." The list here is potentially very long.

3. There's also the personal performance. Three immediately come to mind; all took place at the English Institute in the 1980s: Terry Eagleton wearing a T-shirt and singing a song about the canon to the tune of "Pomp and Circumstance"; Jane Gallop wearing a skirt made out of men's ties and delivering a talk sitting on a table, crossing and uncrossing her legs; Leo Bersani in a sublime white linen suit quoting Sade, and saying fuck (in translation) many times.

4. In the late sixties, the Dutch historian Jacques Presser, in the course of his research about the persecution of the Jews in the Netherlands, coined the term "egodocuments" to describe the range of documents he utilized in his work. He defined this material as "those documents in which an ego intentionally reveals or conceals itself" (286). The term was adopted by feminist historians inspired by research undertaken by the International Women's Archives. Mineke Bosch offers this definition of ego (or personal) documents: "all kinds of documents [diaries, autobiographies, memoirs, scrapbooks and personal letters] in which women present themselves as subjects, mostly in the first person" (166).

In some ways autobiographical criticism, in its desire for self-representation, can be understood as the "egodocuments" of contemporary criticism's archives as well as more material for the history of feminist theory. I should add for its foes that the term "ego" in Dutch has less of a psychoanalytic (hence negative?) connotation than it does in English, and is simply the equivalent of "self." I am grateful to Anneke Smelik for bringing this term to my attention, and for her translation of the Presser definition.

5. In a first rough cut, it does seem, however, that like the narratives of feminist consciousness for women, the anecdote, revived and reauthorized most recently by the new historicism, but long a rhetorical staple of a whole range of discursive practices (brilliantly analyzed by Joel Fineman in his "History of the Anecdote"), has been a way for some men to experiment with self-representation while writing critical theory. But the use of anecdote also characterizes the essays of black women writers like Alice Walker and June Jordan, so one will have to resist the temptation to gender the anecdote—including, of course, my own.

6. Reflecting (in 1976) upon the need for "critical self-discovery," Cary Nelson remarks: "That does not mean that we should make criticism more personal. The decision to add personality to criticism usually results in preciosity or hysteria" ("Reading Criticism," 803).

And in a recent critique of shows of contemporary art entitled "Three Good Arguments for Less Self-Indulgence," Roberta Smith writes: "A weakness shared by the three artists is that all this borrowing and mixing is not countered with enough originality, or with an originality that goes beyond the niceties of style—which all three artists possess in abundance. A possibly related problem is that of personality, of the autobiographical as a substitute for originality" (the *New York Times*, September 2, 1990). I'm interested in the insistence on originality (uniqueness?) as a form of resistance to the autobiographical. What's odd is the fact that this resistance resembles the recent humanist attacks on feminist criticism as being predictable—by which logic the individual becomes as vulnerable as the collective. But what grounds the criteria of originality?

7. On the "masculist" vs. "feminist" understandings of the relations between public authority and private disclosure, Gayatri Spivak observes: "It is not enough to permit the private to play in the reservations marked out by the subdivisive energy of critical labor: the olympian or wryly self-deprecatory touch of autobiography in political polemic or high journalism. It might, on the contrary, be necessary to show the situational vulnerability of a reading as it shares its own provenance with the reader" ("Finding Feminist Readings in Dante-Yeats," 15).

8. This cuts at least two ways. One could argue that the reading effect depends on the status of the writer. No one would care if Jane Doe went to the bathroom: it matters that Jane Tompkins is a known critical quantity, that (some) people will know that she is married to Stanley Fish. And in that sense, the authority effect remains intact (even if some readers are turned off). And indeed, Roland Barthes, in one of his many riffs on writing gives us a piece of self-portrait in *Roland Barthes by Roland Barthes* that quite casually includes "the bathroom"—French style—in a long list of diversionary strategies to avoid writing when in the country: "spray a mosquito, cut my nails, eat a plum, take a piss [aller pisser], check the faucet," etc. (71). But no one, I think, would fuss about Barthes, and this I think is a matter of gender. I'm therefore inclined to maintain that any woman critic "going" would evoke these hostile reactions.

9. Including my own. I rehearse my debt to Barthes in the introduction to *Subject to Change*.

10. In "But What Do We Think We're Doing Anyway" Christian explains that the introduction to "Black Feminist Criticism" was by its moves—"call and response, jazz riffs, techniques found in writers like Hughes and Hurston, as well as the anecdote, a device I had found so effective in the essays of Jordan and Walker"—a way "of reflecting on [her] own process" (68).

11. When I gave this essay as a lecture at Queen Mary and Westfield College, one of the students in the audience strenuously objected to Tompkins's reading of Foucault. Foucault, he claimed used "we" ironically in his argument about the stories "we" have been told. (Here he follows MacLean who argues that Foucault's "we" "is surely a strategic 'we' that seeks to implicate us in the prudery . . . that imperialism necessitates" (146). Rereading Foucault's opening moves in *The History of Sexuality* now in the light of the student's complaint, I would be inclined to introduce a nuance in the analysis of his use of pronouns that supports both the student's view and Tompkins's reaction. Foucault does distinguish between the collective "we" of Western sexual subjects and the singular (though not, to be sure, autobiographical) "I" of his project: *his* will to know as opposed to "our" blindness about the truth of sexuality. But he does not in this volume (as he will in the introduction to the second volume) distinguish between the differentiated positionings of male and female subjects. And this has the effect of putting me at a distance from the community of desire invoked. The insistence on the constitutive role played by gender in any analysis of power relations, of course, is one that Benjamin and other feminist theorists include within their point of departure. In her claims for a more personal voice in writing, Tompkins does not—as MacLean will point out—invoke feminist paradigms as a counterweight to Foucault's generalizations. For more on Foucault and gender, see Naomi Schor's "Dreaming Dissymmetry."

12. This claim for the interest the emotions hold for women echoes Lawrence Lipking's claims for a female "poetics of need" or Carol Gilligan's ethic of care.

13. This is cited in Culler's account of "Reading as a Woman." Heilbrun is in many ways an exception to the rule (of impersonal writing), and a precursor, for she has always written in a nonacademic voice for a wide audience; she also has an important autobiographical discussion in *Reinventing Womanhood* (1978) about being a feminist and an outsider in academic institutions.

14. I am bracketing his observations about Messer-Davidow's project in order to keep the focus on Tompkins, but two remarks are in order here: first that his language is closer to Messer-Davidow's than to Tompkins's; second that both are vulnerable to his grading mode: "Significantly, both of you ignore the work of Gayatri Spivak, which offers the most forceful critique of the philosophical bases of feminist criticisms" (144). Etc. I am also not taking into account the self-narrative MacLean produces within the reply: the account of his relations with his mother and his wife which leads to the confession of having struck his wife during an argument.

15. In his reply to Patricia Yaeger's "Toward a Female Sublime," Lee Edelman makes

the point: "I am uncomfortable with the image of our prom-night pairing that requires this dialogue to reproduce the spectacle of heterosexual coupling" (216). And then goes on to place himself anecdotally as a homosexual critic within the text of his essay (220–22).

16. I am tempted, for instance, to depersonalize the author, separating his name from his text, and dubbing him UF, another unfriendly reader. But in an essay on personal criticism, that might seem really unfriendly, which is not my intention. And this is indeed one of the stickiest problems of personal criticism: responding to the person being personal. "I need to be liked," MacLean writes, "perhaps because I was brought up by a single parent after my father left when I was three" (150). What if I—implied reader, or narratee—not knowing the person, don't like the persona? Am I "right" (he's unlikable, a bad writer), or am I in turn, a UF? I want to say: nothing personal, I don't know you. To what extent is this a *new* problem, or merely an old problem made harder? Does this version of critical embodiment alter or merely bring to light the attractiveness/ unattractiveness of any critical persona, however impersonal?

17. Kipnis analyzes the complexities of this moment in "Feminism: The Political Conscience of Postmodernism?"

18. In "Lesbian Identity and Autobiographical Difference[s]," Biddy Martin summarizes the argument "of several feminist critics [notably Teresa de Lauretis] who read recent autobiographical writings by women of color in the United States as 'representational practices' that illuminate the 'contradictory, multiple construction of subjectivity'"; proposing "a new imbrication of theory and personal history" (82). This is where the materialist-feminist attention to the markings of cultural difference and a poststructuralist take on "différance" (Culler's formulation of "reading as a woman" [43–64]) may be seen to intersect.
On the difference feminism makes to the postmodern moment, see Nancy Hartsock's "Rethinking Modernism: Minority vs. Majority Theories."

19. Two further remarks of Heath's on the personal, masculinity, and theory interest me here: "There *is* a female impersonation in a man reading as a feminist, whatever else there might be too. To think otherwise is to abstract the personal (and that much modern theory is keen on such abstraction says something politically about that theory)"(28); and a distinction—named but not worked out—between "the theoretical," not necessarily marked out by gender, and *"theory* with all its reservations" (12) which is. What feminist theory has shown, precisely, is the unsuspected range of the theoretical: including, importantly, the personal.

20. I am grateful to Abigail Solomon-Godeau for our conversations about feminism and postmodernism. Solomon-Godeau goes so far as to claim postmodernism as a subset of feminism, which is an intriguing reversal of assumptions.

21. It's not the mere mention of the bathroom, although we could also think here about the displacement at work in the phrase "going to the bathroom," a middle-class euphemism to begin with. No eyebrows were raised at Brownstein's earlier account of bathroom reading in "My Life in Fiction"; then again, in Brownstein's scene the heroine

is sitting on a closed seat. At work in the hostile reactions, I think, is a woman's calling attention to herself (and repeating the passage for emphasis) in precisely a domain previously unmarked by gender *in criticism*, but at the same time a gesture historically— on at least typically—in literature represented only in the masculine. Wittig's micturating female subjects in *Les Guérillères* is one exception here, although things are beginning to change on the mass cultural front—Almodóvar's *Tie Me Up, Tie Me Down*, for instance. There was also an ad for Vittel mineral water shown before movies in France this year which represents a man entering a miniature chalet in an idyllic landscape— and zipping himself up with that very particular hitch of self-restoration as he exits. The woman's version has her more vaguely readjusting her shorts.

Other examples that come to mind of reader upset with personal body language include reactions to Alice Walker's praise of her "thighs (which are otherwise gorgeous, and of which I am vain)" ("*One* Child," 366); and generally to Eve Sedgwick's production of a discourse around "female anal eroticism" ("A Poem," 110).

22. And here I need to make my own avowal—as redundant in a sense as Tompkins's— of the currents of my own anger at MacLean's condescension in manner and tone toward women, and, at the same time, the constraints on me not to let it show-- or show too much. In a response to an earlier version of this essay, a friend writes: "I found myself more sympathetic to MacLean than you are and worried about your aggression (is this my fear of female anger against men? probably)."

But a good deal of righteous rhetorical anger is admissible in the attack/reply modes of a journal like, say, *Critical Inquiry*.

For a fuller discussion of gender and anger, see Brenda Silver's "The Authority of Anger: *Three Guineas* as Case Study."

23. On the nature of this contractual relation, see Philippe Lejeune's *On Autobiography*.

24. On a lighter, but not necessarily less serious note, this might be one way of reading Susan J. Leonardi's "Recipes for Reading." "I also wonder," she writes at the end of her article, "if, like Irma Rombauer, I can prompt you, the readers, to respond; if, by speaking the language of the recipe, I can invite answers to these questions for inclusion in my subsequent, revised editions. Will you, as a result of my attempt at recipe sharing, find it easier to argue with me, to point out better examples than the ones I have used, to send me stories, heartwarming or heartburning, about recipe sharing?" (347). I thank Mary Ann Caws for this suggestion.

25. Although I did not know this woman "personally," I met her once in an academic context. She had a great many friends within the profession—many of whom were also friends of mine. Her death, while by most accounts a matter of her personal history and not professional trauma, raised many painful questions about visibility and degrees of individual or collective responsibility within the profession and cast a very long shadow.

2

Untitled Work,
Or, Speaking as a Feminist . . .

This talk was written for a panel discussion called "Creating Feminist Works," which was part of "The Scholar and the Feminist" conference held at Barnard College in 1978, and sponsored by the Barnard College Women's Center (then directed by Jane Gould). The other panelists were Harmony Hammond, painter and a founding member of the Heresies collective, and Eve Merriam, poet and playwright.

Until the occasion of the Barnard conference I had only given talks in panels at meetings like NEMLA, or at small eighteenth-century conferences like NEASECS, where the audience ranged from maybe eleven to a half-empty room of twenty-four (with at least one asleep). Here were hundreds of women, wide awake, or so it seemed, packed into the gym on a Saturday morning. I had been asked to speak as a feminist scholar (as opposed to feminist artists), but we had also been asked to speak personally. And so I tried, in this my first truly occasional piece of writing, to find a tone as close as I could get to my own voice in public in which to talk about my situation as a beginning assistant professor working at becoming a feminist critic and a theorist; and threaded through, about a woman whose personal life was a mess. For a long time I didn't count this piece as part of my "real" work. After the fact—the excitement of the occasion: Reader, remember, this was still the seventies!—the piece embarrassed me, and I didn't put it on my c.v.[1] It is dated, of course, but that may be its greatest value. I sometimes think now that I'm moving backwards in time to join it.[2]

If Eve feels uncomfortable in academia, I feel uncomfortable being
the academic flanked by two artists. And I'm not at all sure that what
I have to say is not permeated with PD values.[3] I'd like to begin with
a few lines from an essay on women's writing by Hélène Cixous entitled
"The Laugh of the Medusa."

> Listen to a woman speak at a public gathering (if she hasn't painfully lost
> her wind). She doesn't "speak" . . . all of her passes into her voice, and
> it's with her body that she vitally supports the "logic" of her speech.
> . . . She lays herself bare. In fact, she physically materializes what she's
> thinking; she signifies it with her body. In a certain way she *inscribes* what
> she's saying, because she doesn't deny her drives the . . . impassioned part
> they have in speaking. Her speech, even when "theoretical" or political,
> is never simple or linear or "objectified," generalized: she draws her story
> into history (251).

We have been asked to speak personally today. Personally, but not
idiopathically. We have been asked, if I may rehearse the request, to
inscribe that rhetorical figure women writers are said to manipulate so
inadequately—the synecdoche, making the part stand for the whole.
A first handicap. Academics, moreover, have the reputation of being
poor "personal" speakers: they confuse the account of a working life
with a *curriculum vitae*. I will try to overcome that second handicap
by saying something—at least for starters—about the grid through
which I perceive my work, and the metaphors of the working process,
the work in progress.

It is the fashion in French literary circles—by which I am vicariously
contaminated—to inquire of a speaker (or, if one is the speaker, to
identify) the locus of one's discourse, to name the place out of which
one speaks; or as they are said to say in California, to say where one
is coming from. It is no less common in feminist circles—at least since
Virginia Woolf—to transcode the metaphor and to speak of one's
space. And that is where I shall begin.

I live in a one-bedroom apartment. The one bedroom in question
has been separated into equal areas by a room divider of standing
bookcases. On one side of the divide is my bed and my TV. On the
other, my desk, more bookcases, and a reading chair. A telephone

negotiates that awkward partition, as does my body. I devised this obstacle course so that I would not have to look at my books when I went to sleep and woke up; and the obvious corollary, so that I would not be able to see my bed from my desk.

What bearing does this have upon creating feminist works?

I don't know exactly. In fact, I would be hard-pressed to determine whether I am speaking as a feminist, a woman, an academic, a writer, or your garden variety neurotic. Nevertheless, the topography has everything to do with my *experience* of what I do. I battle to establish a balance of power between the two major poles of my life: my bed and my desk. I have a room of my own then, but that room is inhabited by two wary antagonists: vertical Professor Miller, who sits at her desk and writes "productively"; and horizontal Nancy who watches television from her bed and mainlines into the telephone. On a good day, the pair does not seem incompatible: the bed is occupied for a legitimate eight hours; the desk for a virtuous five; and all is right both in the room and with the world. On bad days, however, that ratio is skewed resolutely in favor of the bed: the typewriter is routed by TV programs too appalling to name in public; and Professor Miller, that recent and fragile construct, becomes a faint and guilty memory vanquished by an archaic and hence more powerful adversary. I will return in closing to my room and to my war, but for a moment I would like to talk about what I do when I'm vertical.

When Elizabeth Minnich asked me to participate in this panel, I was in the process of teaching my first overtly feminist course, and writing my first overtly feminist criticism. What that means in terms of teaching is that after several years of trying—as discreetly as possible—to subvert the unconscious assumptions of undergraduate men in required courses at Columbia College, I was teaching graduate and undergraduate women in a course devoted to French women writers. At the same time, I was finishing an essay on French women autobiographers. I mention these curricular items to both situate myself for you in time, and to explain—to you and to myself—what led me to take the mildly anxiety-producing step of speaking here today about my activities as a feminist critic. Anxiety-producing not so much because I have never spoken in public—I have been to the conferences that preceded this one and I even ran one—but because I know from experience that someone always says, "Nothing new, we've heard that before." My paranoia—the most prevalent form of psychopathology at Columbia— is such that I have already anticipated that someone will say that today. Let me state then from the outset that I am prepared to assume my belatedness. Being here is anxiety-producing too because I have extremely mixed feelings about what it may or may not mean to be a feminist critic.

So why did I accept? I could cite my megalomania or my masochism. But I think that, in the final analysis, I accepted for metonymic reasons—to float another figure. I accepted on the assumption that I was probably very much like other feminist critics, and why shouldn't I, as well as another, say how I perceived that struggle, since struggle it is.

In an afternoon's workshop at last year's conference entitled "The Need for Feminist Literary Theory," Elaine Showalter made a distinction between feminist critique and feminist criticism that I would like to take up briefly again today. Roughly speaking, under the rubric of feminist critique come those studies of literature that focus on texts of male authors—the better to uncover and demythify the workings of what in France is now called phallocentric discourse. My own published work comes under that heading. As opposed to feminist critique, feminist criticism takes as its object writing by women. Its project is both archaeological and re-evaluative—the better to reclaim and reread the specifically female inscriptions of culture. I have tried in my recent work, both in the classroom and at the typewriter, to say something about the specificity of women's writing. The experience has given me pause.

If a person whose function in this world is *not* to be a literary critic decides to read a work by a woman writer, that person has only to decide whether s/he likes the work in question. If, however, the reader, not having Virginia Woolf's recommended income of 500 pounds a year, earns her living by writing and talking about texts in an institution (of higher learning), that reader has a rather more arduous task to perform. That reader, as she inscribes the critical act within the academy, must not only justify the choice of the work in the first place (because most women's writing has no obvious—i.e., canonical—claim to consideration), but if she is to survive, she must also for political and intellectual reasons be prepared to say something about the writing *qua* women's writing. This is the stumbling block and a particularly awkward one to bypass.

One begins with the assumption that women's lives are different from men's in some irreducible way—a bottom-line assumption as far as I'm concerned—and that this difference would have to affect imaginative structures in some material, hence decipherable way. One then begins to look for the inscription of difference. I was engaged upon that quest with my students last fall when Elizabeth Minnich asked me to speak; and I thought mid-term, in a moment of hubris and extraordinary naiveté, that when the semester was over, an answer, if not *the* answer, would be in sight. It was not. At best I can say that we had a close encounter of the third kind: we all felt that something was out there; it was flashing at us even if we could not present *empirical* evidence which would attest to the existence of another world, another experience, and most important another modality of language. What we did not arrive at was a consensus as to the nature of the encounter, nor what might *govern* the imaginative and linguistic processes of the inhabitants of that world. That twin failure was exceedingly disheartening. For how were we to produce a theory when we could barely articulate what it was that we had experienced?

Let me backtrack a moment to the critique/criticism opposition. When in the performance of critique I work on men's texts, I proceed as though I were confronted with an artichoke. I slowly and systematically remove the leaves, cut away the prickly choke, until I arrive at the heart. This patient removal of layers is rewarded by the overdetermined discovery of the core. What could be more gratifying? Once the artichoke is dismantled, you can see what you have, and you can describe it: textual politics. When I work on women's texts, I begin as though I were dealing with an artichoke, but I must confess that by the time I've finished, I generally feel that my artichoke has turned into an onion. The layers are indeed there, but what is at the center?[4]

35

The desire in me to theorize is not unlike the impulse to "artichoke," if I may coin a verb. And to be interrogated. The notion of stripping away layers is after all associated in our culture with a male erotic: strip tease. The final layer, veil, or piece to fall away is the *cache-sexe*, the secular fig leaf. Therefore, to "go with" the artichoke metaphor—which I freely inflicted upon myself—is to embrace a "masculinist" analysis. To the extent that different texts call for different modalities of reading, it is not surprising that the phallocentric text elicits a practice that both reveals and reduces. Therefore, it is perfectly inevitable that, given my training, I should "get off" on the artichoke and its heart. To feel at ease with the onion, to enjoy its onion-ness, would mean accepting a radical decentering and reorganization of pleasure: finding pleasure not in the revelation of a center, but in the process itself of the peeling away of layers.

But anyone who has ever dealt with an onion in what my parents like to call the "real world" has already perceived the inherent flaw in my opposition. For while an onion is indeed constituted by layers, beyond removing the brittle outer skin, one does not peel onions. To perceive that an onion has layers, one has to cut into it, slice, chop, or dice; and for those incisions, as we well know, one pays the price of tears.

What I am trying to bring out here in lieu of a conclusion is quite simple. It is this: that the articulation of difference cannot be undertaken with old metaphors and familiar recipes. Yet for the time being, I have found no new ones that work to my satisfaction.

I have found no new metaphors, that is, metaphors I can announce in public, mainly I think because I am hooked, as Honor Moore has diagnosed the matter so accurately in *Polemic #1*, on the "male approval desire filter" (abbreviated M-A-D), which, as she puts it, "instructs by quiet magic women to sing proper pliant tunes for father, lover, piper who says he has the secret." (I have had to mutilate the line for my argument, but my apologies.)[5] It is this same M-A-D again that makes me feel skeptical about onions, anxious about theorizing, and nostalgic for my artichoke days. I would like to respond to Honor's

Untitled Work

call for "poems, women"; and to take down my room divider, my cordon sanitaire. I would like to, but am I ready for détente?[6]

NOTES

1. Not only because it was personal in style, but because the writing came out of an unhappiness I hoped was behind me (what reads as irony began as pathos).

2. I began the retrieval process by excerpting a paragraph from it in the introduction to *Subject to Change*.

My parents came to hear me speak. My mother, who had proofread my dissertation a few years earlier and pointed out with some irritation that any number of words I used were not in the dictionary, seized the opportunity to ask why I didn't write like this more often; why I didn't write something for the *New York Times Magazine*, for instance (the ultimate reference for middle-class New Yorkers). I was (as I always seemed to be in those days) absolutely infuriated—would they never understand what I was trying to do?—and of course now, I can't think of anything I would rather do more, and that is less likely to happen!

3. In the opening moves of her talk, in attempting to define what art could be defined as feminist—the charge of the conference—Merriam began, as a way of mapping the territory of the discussion, by describing *non*-feminist work, work that "adheres to patriarchally determined values. The shorthand for patriarchally determined," she explained, "is 'PD'" (12). Its rules are "paid, published and praised by the male establishment" (13).

4. After the conference, Peggy Waller, one of the students from my course on French women writers (Fall 1977) [now assistant professor of French at Pomona College], brought to my attention the existence of an onion metaphor which predates my own: "If, until now we have looked at the text as a species of fruit with a kernel (an apricot, for example), the flesh being the form and the pit being the content, it would be better to see it as an onion, a construction of layers (or levels, or systems) whose body contains, finally, no heart, no kernel, no secret, no irreducible principle, nothing except the infinity of its own envelopes—which envelop nothing other than the unity of its own surfaces" (Barthes, "Style," 10). The artichoke remains mine.

5. The line continues: ". . . but wants ours; it teaches us to wear cloaks labelled/ Guinevere, become damsels, objects in men's power joustings/like her: lets us shimmer, disappear, promise to rise like a/Lady of the Lake, but we drown—real, not phantom."

6. I want to thank Jane Opper for her editorial work on the earliest versions of this paper.

37

3

A Feminist Teacher in the Graduate Classroom

I. Mastery, Identity, and the Politics of Work

This paper was conceived for a program at MLA 1980 arranged by the Division on Women's Studies in Language and Literature. Entitled "Feminist Pedagogy: Positions and Points of View," it was presided over by Judith Fetterley and Elaine Marks; the other panelists were Carolyn Allen, Evelyn Beck, and Hortense Spillers.

Like "Untitled Work," this piece bears its date in history: my own, speaking as an assistant professor at the threshold of the tenure process; and feminism's, the debate over the status of "male" theory.

Let me begin by identifying the political realities that have generated the chain of abstractions structuring the title of my paper. For the context of my local situation has everything to do with my general sense of what is possible or desirable in the feminist pedagogic enterprise and may help to explain the slightly depressive tone of my reflection. I am speaking, then, as a feminist teacher engaged for one-fifth of her time in the education of (primarily) women within the walls and wisdom of an elite institution originally organized by men for the education of men; a teacher, moreover, performing in a classroom in which she herself was a graduate student in the more euphoric moments of the early 1970s: post '68.

In 1980, the study of French literature at Columbia University is still a pursuit undertaken primarily by women in a department run by men committed to theorizing the theory of literature. What has changed—at Columbia and elsewhere, of course—is neither the privileged discourse, nor the familiar ecology of power, but the sheer numbers of the unempowered: there are fewer graduate students, with less money to sustain them, and fewer jobs to dream of. These demographic and economic specificities mean, for starters, that the paranoia always inherent in hierarchical organizations is now aggravated by an equally real and altogether appropriate anxiety about survival. What, in such a situation, is an appropriate feminist pedagogy?

What is it, I ask myself, I think I am doing by encouraging these women to continue (or begin) working for a degree that will theoretically entitle them to bear the title of professor? Am I not encouraging them to "imitate" me —under conditions far less favorable to their success? Perhaps this peculiar form of female narcissism—a term more apt, I think, than the cooler and sociological notion of "role modeling" to describe the psychic miming at the heart of this doubling—is not only irresponsible but wrong. Perhaps a talented young woman should *not* be encouraged to embrace the conditions of a profession agonizing under threat of continued attrition in the humanities, not to mention the wages of what has been called affirmative inaction. Would she not be better off doing something else altogether? Or at least, if determined to run the risk, should she run it as a feminist? I believe this is called double jeopardy. My answer to that well-known dilemma has been to take in my person the willfully naive but no less self-conscious leap of faith that embodies the belief that it is possible to bring about difference despite repetition, that it is indeed possible to bring about change because without that wager we guarantee that no change will occur at all. This is part of what I mean by the politics of work: and why, no less obviously, we are all here at this forum.

In the classroom as a feminist teacher, therefore, I maintain—if only by my presence there—that one can survive the vicissitudes of a feminist destiny inside the private patriarchal bailiwick I have described. There is, however, one crucial precondition: that this critical identity be perceived as strong within the terms of institutional practice. This may sound a resolutely conservative politics to be proposing under the name of feminist pedagogy, but I believe that I owe my own survival (thus far) as a "woman who works on women" (as I have come to be known) on the fifth floor of Philosophy Hall (there is a copy of Rodin's *Thinker* in front of the building) to the fact that I was also originally perceived as a structuralist.[1] Today, for graduate students in French post-structuralist times and fiefdoms, other perceptions obtain. But whatever the methodological engagements, a feminist mastery of phallocentric mysteries is, I think, an essential strategy for survival. This does not, of course, mean believing that the truth inhabits those systems; rather, it is to recognize that their limits cannot be located within an understanding of their claims to the truth.

I hope it is clear, then, that I understand feminist mastery as a subversive move and not as a gesture of docile complicity and ideological collusion.[2] I have in mind a double move of appropriation that both meets the master narratives on their own grounds and refuses them as the only grounds of theoretical power. What I seek to do in the classroom, therefore, is to expose at all times the blind spots in the dominant codes (and modes) of meta-critical discourse as they are pressed into the service of a feminist analysis. This exposure is meant to detheatricalize the scenarios of mastery and to raise the curtains on the stage of its production. In that process, ideally, the classroom becomes not a showcase for exhibitionistic intimidation, but a scene of work.

I shall give one concrete example of this practice. I offered an interdisciplinary course last spring called "Studies in French Eighteenth-Century Fiction and Painting: Ideologies of Representation." The title was deliberately ponderous and vague, designed to deliver a preemptive strike on the Committee on Instruction. What I wanted to do was to look at—literally and figuratively—the inscriptions of the sexual and social relations between the sexes in eighteenth-century texts. I pretty much knew what I would find— the territory, after all, was not entirely unknown to me—but two pedagogic anxieties immediately emerged: how to present the material (a practical problem); and in what language or meta-language to articulate the findings (a theoretical or methodological problem). The second anxiety was particularly acute since despite the political blandness of the course title, I was teaching from a feminist perspective students—some of whom were men—who did not all necessarily conceive of themselves as feminists in their work or in their lives. I wanted even more acutely to perform a remapping of the territory that would prevent feminist analysis from appearing—to the skeptical—to be a thematics. I wanted, I confess, to seduce.

Paradoxically, though I have no training in art history (and machine anxiety to boot), showing slides and "reading" paintings proved to be the most persuasive tool I had ever used in teaching. Sitting in the darkened room, watching the obsessions of the century—the visual fantasies of the Enlightenment's erotic imagination—it was impossible not to see what lay behind the fictions of desire in the age of reason. The results of this unveiling were compelling in two ways: in the first instance, it brought woman's body—in various stages of undress— physically into the classroom; in the second (a consequence of the first), it identified all of us in the room as gendered and sexual beings— whether we wanted to be identified in that way or not. It was a kind of enactment of the inescapable relations between bodies and theories, the intersections of the personal and the political.

I do not mean to suggest that looking at slides has any inherently feminist value to it, or that an interdisciplinary offering necessarily leads to feminist epiphanies. What I am claiming is that this particular teaching situation—in which I was forced to let go of my own fragile claims to mastery by virtue of taking on the visual—allowed me to bring out into the open the stakes of theorization itself. In the absence of adequate models for articulating the relations between visual and verbal texts, the politics of the image and the erotics of reading, we had to forge our own, building from the strategies available to us, devising new ones at the scene of their failure. Because, as I have been saying, I think it is crucial for women and for feminist scholarship to have a less mystified relation to mastery and theory, I feel that the experiment was both demonstrative and exhilarating.

That is not, however, the whole story. By relinquishing the standard peacock model of graduate teaching, designed to dazzle the hens, in favor of a more ambiguous and less predictable pedagogy, I ran the

41

risk of losing my own identity as the teacher—the one who is supposed to know—and the guaranteed seduction that strutting (one's stuff) traditionally effects. That risk is neatly defined in Nietzsche's aphorism: "We don't believe that the truth still remains the truth once its veil has been removed" (in Baudrillard, *On Seduction*, 85). Though there were students who did seem to believe that, in the end, an empowering discourse would have to come from within—not naively, of course, but from patient negotiations with competing claims to authority—I have the distinct impression that there were students who would have preferred for me to remain veiled, for identity to remain seamless, for mastery to remain mystifying. I do not know of course whether their resistance to my unveiling was due to a resistance to a more collaborative pedagogy, or to an inadequacy inherent in the project itself. Perhaps what I took to be their nostalgia for the peacock is merely a projection of my own ambivalence. The desire for the master's voice is not to be underestimated.

In any event, this, I think, is the question of feminist pedagogy in the graduate classroom: how to create a critical identity which understands the discourses of mastery without succumbing to their seductions? For seduced, we are simply the old slaves, or worse, the new masters. In closing, it is not clear to me what metaphorical bird to oppose to the peacock. Just us chickens? Nor what erotic model to oppose to the old power politics of seduction and betrayal. It is clear, however, that through the recognition of same to same, despite the mark of difference always inscribed by hierarchy, new identities do emerge. And that is, after all, one of the tasks and joys of any pedagogy.

II. "Teaching the Two Georges"

In the fall of 1988 Rachel Brownstein and I taught a course on George Sand and George Eliot together at the CUNY Graduate Center that we always referred to familiarly by its subtitle as: "The Two Georges." The seminar, however, which was listed both in the English and the Comparative Literature programs, had titles that would look more serious on the transcript: "Studies in Prose Fiction" (Comp. Lit.) and "Writing Women in the Nineteenth Century" (English). For the special session that Naomi Schor organized at the MLA that year "Reading the Two Georges: Sand, Eliot, and the Making of Feminist Canons," we each wrote a short paper in which we tried separately to describe what was at stake for us in the bringing together of two writers who both touch and pull apart on so many points of authorship. At the session, Schor gave a paper on Sand's processes of idealization; Christina Crosby *on Eliot's idealism in* Daniel Deronda.

I knew at the time—although I didn't have the room in so short a take (ten minutes!) to include the reflection as a subject in itself—that I was also reviewing the arguments rehearsed earlier in "Mastery, Identity, and the Politics of Work," in which I had tried to come to terms with the vexing issue of the place of Theory in feminist classrooms within patriarchal—what other word is there, finally?—academic organizations. Reading over the two pieces together now what strikes me is the persistence of my ambivalence on the subject despite the differences—not addressed here—in the institutional context of the teaching and the writing about it. When I wrote "Mastery, Identity" in 1980, I was speaking as an assistant professor in the throes of tenure anxiety and teaching at a private institution. By the time I wrote "Teaching the Two Georges," I had become a tenured professor and had begun teaching in a public institution. Although these changes in status have certainly complicated my experience of institutional constraints, what hasn't changed for me is an uncertainty about what feminist graduate students need to know in order to survive in a profession that still resists mightily the seriousness of feminist work and theory: what is it that they need to master? What is it that I, from my supposed position of mastery, should be conveying to them? In a seminar on female authorship, for instance, should one begin with "The Death of the Author" *or* Madwoman in the Attic? *Or both?*

In a way, then, the anxiety I rehearse here about what "they" should know has more to do with debates within feminism about what constitutes theory than whether or not the seminar was successful

(which from my point of view it wasn't fully, at least in its own terms).
It also has to do with my own attachment to the revisionary poetics
with which I constructed my own reading strategies. Perhaps this is a
model itself in need of revision.

Because the presentation of the MLA talk, like the seminar itself,
involved Rachel Brownstein's essential collaboration, I am sorry not
to be able to include her view (the other ten minutes) of the Georges
here.

So what were we doing with our two Georges?

This is what we said we were doing when we had to make up a blurb
for advertising the course:

> In the seminar we will consider George Eliot and George Sand as major
> writers and significant presences in nineteenth-century culture—both their
> contributions to intellectual life and the ways in which they became social
> figures. The juxtaposition of the two writers will allow us to explore
> differences between English and French attitudes toward gender and art.
> In addition to selected novels, we will read poetry, essays, autobiography,
> and letters by both writers, as well as recent biographies and criticism.
> Theoretical readings will address questions of genre and gender.

In what follows, you will hear how we did and didn't fulfill this
agenda.

We called this a study of the woman writer as a *figure*, by which we
meant at the beginning a variety of not very well articulated things.
First, most simply, both Sand and Eliot were in their times and are still
today figures of the national imagination, and indeed in the case of
Sand, international imaginaries: the name George Sand has real recognition value (to invoke the language of marketing), even if what the
name conjures, in the United States, at least, is a woman who wore
trousers and smoked cigars, slept with Chopin and probably lots of
others, while being busily frigid—all on public television. George Eliot's name evokes less colorful (less bodily) images abroad; in the
United States, she is most commonly thought of, by non-academic

44

audiences, at least, as an eminent Victorian and the author of *Silas Marner*, required reading in American high schools.

We started from that sense of figure, however mythified, and tried to recuperate to our own ends each writer's public identity. We argued that through their fictions each writer created a cultural *persona* that she named by a pseudonym, and that finally the social and historical reception of those signatures become the "truth" of their identities. We started with the assumption that although clearly neither of the Georges would have imagined her life and works being studied in a university, or have wanted to be read as a woman novelist, for us reading *as feminist critics* both Georges could be seen to articulate, not to say embody, in their writing a desire to find a voice of authority beyond the gender of their persons: a desire that as its effect produced (paradoxically, or inevitably) the mark of gender in their work. Reading for the women behind the Georges, we were especially interested in the ways in which the so-called "flaws" of their writing—authorial intrusion, philosophizing, implausibility—seemed intextricably bound up with the cultural constraints of gender and misogyny; we read the ambivalence and oscillation in their various narrative personae as a distancing from gender identification, textual displacements of a powerful desire to attain a universal truth and reception. (This is in my language what Rachel theorized in more theatrical terms.)

We wanted to track this effect of the figure in a variety of ways: in the positioning, for instance, of the gaze in writing—the ambiguously gendered narrator watching the man looking at the woman: Stephen Guest fascinated by Maggie's arm, Daniel Deronda scrutinizing Gwendolen at the gambling table, and more complicated still, Musset contemplating Sand's creation of Raymon looking at Noun; and Pulcheria gazing at the sleeping Lélia. We contrasted the voices of the fiction and non-fictional prose, including, in Sand's case, an autobiography in letters. We considered the biographies—their fascination with the love lives of the Georges, and the authors' beauty, or lack of it— and offered a critique of the criticism: the terms in which the writing and the author were evaluated. We pointed to cultural contexts, the ways in which their figures as authors continue to be represented (marketed): the photograph, for instance, on the cover of the Sand/Flaubert letters in English translation of the actress, Rosemary Harris, who played Sand on TV. What had readers before us made of the relation (if any) between the two Georges: what did the French George mean to the English one? What did the readers of the English George make of that relation? What did we make of their reading? And most of all, perhaps, we thought about the figure of the Georges in our own construction as feminist readers at the end of the twentieth century.

What did our students make of our project? At each seminar meeting students, in groups of twos, had been assigned to come to class with questions for discussion. Mid-semester, in the course of a student presentation on *The Mill on the Floss* and Eliot's biographers, we got part of the answer. The students began by reviewing some of the early criticism of the novel, in particular biographical criticism of the "Maggie Tulliver is essentially identical with the young Mary Ann Evans we all know" variety that we had been putting forward as exactly what we *didn't* mean by thinking about the "figure" of the woman writer. The students then asked: "Do we accept this as truth?" And then: "Is there any factual basis for seeing Maggie Tulliver as George Eliot? And if so, can we use the life to politicize the work rather than 'domesticating' it as has been done in the past?" What struck us in the questions was their unmediated seriousness: neither rhetorical, nor theoretical, but expecting an explanation of method of the sort that we clearly had not produced: "How ought," the student presenters went on to wonder, "aspects of the life be brought to bear on the already acknowledged construct of the narrator?" At the next meeting, we took up these questions directly and tried to summarize our project on the figure of the author—as opposed to the narrator *and* the writer—and the ways in which the study of the work could contribute to a de-naturalized notion of the life. We went on and on about the figure—no, *not* the story—until one of our best students said simply: "it's very difficult."

Since that session I've been wondering about her perception. Was the problem an effect of our pedagogy or of the project itself: the two of *us* or the two of them? Probably a little of both. But mainly I think the difficulty came from the contradictions of the present moment in feminist and literary studies. On the one hand, a doxa proclaiming "The Death of the Author," on the other, a commitment to revising the canon by rethinking the work of women writers. For us, the concept of the figure of the author—neither an entirely disembodied writing instance, nor an an originary authority—was a concept designed to negotiate between two lines not meant to cross. The task of feminist cultural studies today involves, I think, the remapping of this space: a place in which to read the complexities of gendered authorship.

Between the truth of intention and the fiction of signature stands this figure of ours that I will call now for lack of a better term, the third George: she's a figure of feminism.

NOTES

1. As it turned out none of this seemed to matter very much. I wasn't kept at Columbia. Does this mean that it is unwise to regard any strategy for (female and feminist) survival in *institutional* terms as anything more than a self-sustaining fiction (fantasy)? Probably. But, if a feminist teacher, whatever the denouement of her own specific plot may be, can bring *other* women along within the *provisional* terms of her tenure, all is not in vain.

2. Moreover, I should also like to make clear here that I do not regard the *production* of theory as masculine in origin. On the contrary. In France today, women intellectuals and writers are producing texts of crucial importance for feminist scholarship: Hélène Cixous, Luce Irigaray, Julia Kristeva—to name just three of the better-known figures theorizing the "feminine."

4

The French Mistake

I wrote "The French Mistake" for a special session at MLA (1988) called "Français impeccable: Memoirs of a Near Native Speaker." This was the spinoff of a project of Alice Kaplan's, who was in the process of writing a book with the working title "Confessions of a Francophile." Kaplan's memoirs excited me because they explored a territory that normally remains closed off from academic discourse: the personal (at least autobiographical) reasons why one "chooses" a field. Since I had been leaving French for a while (the way you stay in a bad marriage), I was tempted by the chance to think about what over the years I had come to dislike the most about being in French.

I say that for the requirements of the genre—explaining why one undertakes an academic project—but I really didn't have to think about it: what I hated most was speaking French because of the anxiety making French mistakes—especially gender mistakes—creates in me. From the response I had to the paper from colleagues, it is clear that I am not alone in these feelings. Because commiseration was palpable in the room when I spoke, I have wanted to hold on to the occasion by leaving the paper unchanged in this book as a form of thanks.

In a paper called "Intellectual Formations," Alice Kaplan spoke about her graduate student days at Yale; in "Thème et version" Naomi Schor described the trajectory (via the Lycée français de New York) of a bi-lingual, near native speaker.

I am a recovering francophile. More specifically a recovering francophonie-o-phile. French has become for me a foreign language; I have given up all aspirations to the world of "français impeccable." Indeed, I have *not* been able to pass for a near native speaker for such a long time that I *only* belong on this panel memorially: taking the title literally, recalling what it was like to be addicted to French and hooked on not making mistakes. I do not mean by this that there was ever a time I didn't make mistakes; making some kind of mistake, is definitionally, the fate of the *near* native speaker. Rather that I used to get hung over from them when I indulged. I was hooked on trying not to make them and caring intensely about whether I and other people did. *Rule 1.* French mistakes always involve other people, whether as witnesses or rivals or compatriots. (A really good French mistake combines all three.) The whole point of the French mistake is that it is intersubjective and social; and like a fart or any other failure of politeness, it never goes unnoticed.

I'll start with something not too bad, a vocabulary mistake: a cognate, or "faux ami" as they are cutely known to teachers of French. The scene is a Chinese restaurant in New York, maybe ten years ago. A group of academics are assembled around the table at a dinner party organized in honor of a visiting Frenchman. This man, next to whom I have been seated, is witty and cutting, and because of this intimidates me: I can't be witty and cutting back—in French. There is much business about passing the food, serving oneself, the French and Chinese food—they don't like to mix salt and sweet—Americans and Chinese food—you get free rice: the usual conversation about cultural commonplaces by academics in French trying to be social with actual French people. At some point, visiting Frenchman finds himself confronted with a serving problem, the details of which escape me: let's say, he wants to help himself to mooshoo pork and there are no serving spoons in sight. Someone suggests that he use his own silverware (he has not mastered chopsticks), and I say, brightly, I hope, helpfully, oh no, VF (visiting Frenchman) wouldn't do that: "il est trop fastidieux." Now VF doesn't have time to wonder why I am accusing him of being tiresome, because my neighbor on the other side, a Francophone and colleague whose fate at our common institution has been played off against mine (a strategy through which both lose), jumps in to clarify: "Mais non," I don't mean "fastidieux," I mean, "pointilleux"

49

(a word whose existence I had until that moment ignored, as they say in French). A fascinating discussion ensues involving everyone at the table about the best translation for "fastidious"; "tatillon," perhaps. I can still remember the feeling of rage I experienced having my French mistake served up for the rest of the meal. (The other day a colleague mentioned having had lunch with VF and I thought: "fastidieux.")

False friends are especially embarrassing to the aspiring near native speaker not only because they are mistakes, but because they reveal unmistakably the speaker's true origin: gone are the hopes of passing one's accent off as regional. Only an American speaker, for instance, would describe a particularly elegant women's room as "la plus belle toilette" of the campus to a visiting Frenchwoman, whom she had accompanied to the very spot; accompanied as well, of course, by the French-mistake counter, who underlines to the baffled visitor, who has been looking in puzzlement at her distinctly frumpy outfit: "*les* plus belles toilettes." Which brings me to another important feature of the French mistake: it is always a mistake one makes for the first time: that is, I had never before turned "toilettes" into the singular. It was the effort to be clever—to entertain the visitor—that derailed me. Moral, that we can return to in the discussion period: never try to have a personality in a foreign language. It will always come back to haunt you.

There isn't time to elaborate a complete taxonomy of French mistakes here—the subjunctive and why real French people make mistakes, too—ditto for agreement of past participles, the pleonastic "ne," etc. These are more complicatedly part of a larger problematics, the refinements of the poetics of passing that I can only allude to— en passant: the imponderables of the liaison; the subtleties of intonation, gestures—shrugging, puffing and sucking air—instead of or as accompaniment to words, where a simple yes or no would do, pouting, etc.

In the time that remains, I'd like to focus instead more specifically on the gender mistake, which I see as the truly fatal and unredeemable mistake. The gender mistake is fatal because no French person makes gender mistakes—at least on common words. (I was telling a French friend about this paper and she said, "but it happens to French people, too," and proceeded to recount an instance in which she was corrected by a friend, a school teacher, for having said incorrectly, "un aphte": "Mais ma chérie, on dit 'une aphte'": and then turned out to be right. But the point, I think, remains.)

I'm going to tell two gender-mistake stories, and here I, like Jean-Jacques confessing Mme de Warens, have to tell the sins of others. Maybe fifteen years ago, a distinguished theoretician of literary studies was lecturing at the *Maison française* of Columbia, the old one on 113th Street, which did feel a little like a French *house*. I do not remember the topic of his lecture, only his mistake. In the process of referring, if memory serves, to a line from Baudelaire's "Correspondances," distinguished critic (from an English department, it should be said in fairness), said: "le forêt." The proverbial pin drops. Eyebrows shoot up. Sidelong glances are exchanged: "*le* forêt." Silent snorts of disapproval: I certainly hope they weren't planning to hire him into the French department. Famous poetician is covered by disgrace; the graduate students yuck it up: "*le* forêt"!! But this is only Part I of famous gender mistakes.

Many years later, last spring in fact, I was at a dinner party—of academics. For reasons that escape me, I found myself telling the anecdote to a group of people, including a French person. As I get to the forest, a horrible, sinking feeling comes over me: "le forêt" or "la forêt"? *le* or *la*? It is as though invoking the category of gender brings back its total arbitrariness: is the forest masculine or feminine? I flail around, desperately praying for a mnemonic boost, trying to think of a fixed phrase with a marked adjective that would rescue me from the rigor of the article: like *maison française:* none comes. I am having a full-fledged gender panic attack. Defeated, I confess my plight to the little group. The story, of course, goes down the tubes, and I am left not only having blown the anecdote, but my cover: having made—while *speaking English*—a gender mistake. Never mind that the French person, after more than ten years in the U.S., still sounds like Maurice Chevalier, I feel covered in shame. Thank God, I think, I'm no longer "in French."

As I write about this for an audience of my colleagues in French I feel tense. I am now compounding my humiliation by telling it again, in a place where these things are taken seriously: the Modern Language Association. Why am I doing this to myself? Playing the foreign-language variant of the game "humiliation" so memorably evoked in that great novel of academic politics, *Changing Places*. Maybe I'm being silly. What difference, someone (not someone in French, of course) might ask, does it make? Well, a gender mistake can cost someone a job. Many years ago, probably around the time of the "le forêt" episode, a brilliant young graduate student whose work I knew and admired was looking for her first job. She had an interview with the search committee of a major mid-western French department. I happened to know, from another incarnation, a man on the hiring committee, and I asked him how her interview went (she really wanted this job and I wanted to be helpful). He said, "Nancy, she doesn't know French." "What do you mean," I said, since I had read her thesis and knew she knew French. "Well," he said, at the interview, "she referred to her dissertation as 'mon thèse.'" "'Mon thèse,'" he repeated in scornful disbelief. In the face of his incredulity—a man who went so far as to marry a Frenchwoman I doubt he was ever in love with in order to perfect his French, but that is another topic—I remember having the mixed feelings the mistakes of others always produce in me. I thought on the one hand—wow, now that's a real mistake—a mistake *I* wouldn't make (especially surprising perhaps because it's the sort of thing one might have rehearsed for a job interview); and there's a sort of awful comfort in feeling superior in that way (this sense of superiority has a lot to do, I think, with the ways in which gifted non-native speakers keep up the tyranny over their colleagues less talented in mimicry). At the same time, it seemed shockingly stupid that a department would not hire a clearly brilliant young person—who has since fulfilled all the promise she showed then—over the question of a gender mistake. I hope they—as I assured them they would—have often eaten their heart out.

SPEAKING WONDERFUL FRENCH. SPEAKING WONDERFUL FRENCH, FOR AN . . . AMERICAN.

You have almost no accent.

His/her French is/isn't very good. He/she speaks wonderful French. She speaks fluently.

Why did I "go" into French? Two memories from junior high school, a formative time. One. I'm called to the phone by my mother. Mrs. Citronbaum—it astonishes me to retrieve these names after thirty-five years with such utter clarity, the mother of a classmate, and a friend of my mother's, wants me to pronounce something in French. Her son Ronny is failing French. She spells out: Q u apostrophe e s t dash c e q u e c apostrophe e s t and sighs hopefully. "Qu'est-ce que c'est?" I say promptly, interested to learn that something that seems obvious to me is a source of mystery to others. Is knowing how to say "qu'est-ce que c'est" important? As good as knowing how to figure out when, if one train leaves Albany at 3 p.m. and travels at fifty miles an hour, and another leaves New York at 4 p.m. and travels at sixty miles an hour, the two trains will meet?

The other: the following year, my grandmother dies. I take a French test and confuse, I think, the passé indéfini and the passé défini. (I've never been able to reconstruct exactly what went on there: it had something to do with tenses; getting thrown by "I went" and "I have gone"—forgetting that they can be the same in French.) In any event, I get a really bad grade—passing, but in the sixties—and I am in shock. I go up to the teacher, whose name I also remember: Mme Neuchatz— her first name, Marie. She is French, of a frowsy, indefinite sort. I tell her, by way of explanation for my poor performance on the test, that my grandmother died. She asks whether my grandmother lived with us. When I say no, she says, then it doesn't count: i.e., the test counts because it doesn't count if your grandmother dies and she doesn't live with you. This turns me off French.

Getting Personal

I have no memories of French in high school. I go to college and start out as an English major. In the summer after my sophomore year, I go, classically, fulfilling my middle-class origins, to Stratford-on-Avon. I meet French students studying Shakespeare in England. This strikes me as brilliant. If I became a French major, I could have a legitimate reason for going to Paris: to work on my French. (I have discovered Europe, before reading *Portrait of a Lady*.)

I set out to learn French again in college. Despite my excitement, I sense that this is a step down, since the smartest students at Barnard, or so I thought, were English majors. At the same time I experience a certain lowering of anxiety: this is concrete, you don't have to be smart to be good in French. Still, I am behind the other French majors and have to take beginning composition with M. Mesnard, who wears a beret and gives D's for grammar mistakes. I go to Middlebury summer school where one signs a pledge not to speak a word of English for six weeks, under the threat of expulsion, and has to make vinaigrette for one's dinner table companions. I go to Vermont twice to "perfect" my spoken French. I discover the fatal connection between French and sex (or at least French professors and American girls). This lasts a long time. I go to France after graduation from college. By then I have read *Portrait*. I marry what I take to be an Osmond look-alike. I get involved in speaking French, eating French, having French health, using *ampoules* at meals, saying "euh" when speaking English. I have a moment of veritable *jouissance* when a French colleague tells me I only make one mistake in pronunciation (a vowel sound, as in "oui"—presumably I say something more like "we"); I didn't know I was making it, and probably still do. I study for a French degree for teaching English. I keep trying to be French.

After six years of trying to be French, I return to the States, my life a shambles. I teach French in a high school. I get through the day alternating between Valium and Ritalin. What should I do? I decide to get a Ph.D., a fate, I had thought of in college as being reserved for men. But this is now 1968. To me a Ph.D. means only "Teaching College" (in our advanced immigrants lingo as distinct from and superior to "teaching high school"); it does not mean what I now refer to

54

as "The Profession." I go to graduate school in French. It does not even occur to me to apply to Yale. I have no idea about these things. I'm "going for the degree" in order to suffer less teaching French, which I'm only doing because I don't know how else to earn a living. Years go by. I become a graduate student and an assistant professor. Being in "The Profession" replaces living in Europe. Being "in French" (as a substitute for being French) seems sexy—if you can imagine finding Structuralism a turn-on (we did). Then things change. I am not "kept" by the Columbia French Department. I cross the street to run the Women's Studies Program at Barnard. I am not invited to join their French department. French drops out of my title. Am I still "in French"? I continue to teach graduate courses in the French department, in English. I speak French less and less. Once a year when I go to Europe.

It's 1986. I have just arrived in Paris on a grant to finish my book on French women writers (secretly to "keep up" my French). I am buying fruit at a vegetable stand in the rue de Buci. I ask for a "livre de pêches." The vegetable lady looks at me and inquires—"deux ou trois." I look back at her blankly. I know I have asked for "une livre" (feeling absolutely confident that I haven't carelessly said "*un* livre"). So why is she asking me two or three? As I wonder, she raises her hand and gestures impatiently with her fingers and repeats: "deux ou trois." Mortified by her charade, it finally dawns on me that she wants to know whether, given the variability of the size of fruit, I want two or three peaches in my pound. I walk home, smarting from the exchange and pondering the state of my French.

It's 1988. I've now become, at least in title, a professor of English, although I'm also welcome to teach in the French program. I discover that contrary to my previous practice (of teaching in my "native" language), one is expected to teach in French. But, no way. I'm not about to teach a graduate course and worry about making French mistakes in front of my students, some of whom are . . . native speakers. This could mean that I won't be teaching for the program again because "tout en français" has become something of an article of faith. Since I am new, they graciously make an exception for me, this one time.

What price French mistakes?

5

Parables and Politics:
Feminist Criticism in 1986

This paper was written for a round-table on feminist scholarship called "Do Women's Studies Make a Difference?" held at Wesleyan University (February 1986) and sponsored by the Women's Studies Program. Panelists were asked to reply to the following charge: "Speculate on the degree to which feminist thinking has changed the objects of study, the methods, the theoretical premises of the discipline within which the feminist scholar works—and perhaps the degree to which the disciplines are practically or theoretically unchanged." The other panelists were Joan W. Scott and Evelyn Fox Keller.

Around this time last year I spoke at a conference sponsored by the Pembroke Center at Brown University. The title of that conference, "Feminism/Theory/Politics," juxtaposed the key words of what I still take to be the crossroads of the current moment, and I have translated them into the title of this paper, adding the element of narrativity that comes along with parables. I spoke then about female subjectivities; the making of feminist critical theory; and about the conditions in which this real-life and fictional project (that I tend to think of as a narrative) could take place.[1] The heroine of that story was Charlotte Brontë's Lucy Snowe, who is, I think, a proper heroine for feminist parables (at least about literary types), since she earns her living in an academic institution that overworks and underpays her for her mastery and teaching of modern languages. (I am particularly, which is to say autobiographically, attracted to Lucy Snowe because she teaches women and knows French.)

But those of you who know *Villette*, the novel in which Lucy performs and writes so brilliantly, will remember that Lucy does not always have an easy time in her apprenticeship to the rigors and conventions of academic life. Indeed, one could argue that to a great extent her *Bildung*, her formation as a speaking and writing subject, can be understood only against the institutional realities that structure her personal situation. Thus if I recur to her in this discussion, it is precisely (if only emblematically) to pick up the struggle that inheres in that relation. What I am concerned with here, then, has a double focus: the work of feminist criticism and its relation to the structuring effects of academic practice in the United States. In other words, the good news and the bad news.

Now in the original good news/bad news jokes, the good news was bad, and the bad news worse; in my own anecdotes, however, the good news is good and the bad bad. Thus, to "speculate on the degree to which feminist thinking has changed the objects of study, the methods, the theoretical premises of the discipline" of literary studies, the good news is that feminist literary scholarship has produced: 1. new objects of study, i.e., women's writing; 2. new strategies of reading—what Adrienne Rich has called "re-vision," "the act of looking back, of seeing with fresh eyes, of entering an old text from a new critical direction" ("When We Dead Awaken," 35); 3. new critical practices which enact or embody the readings, otherwise known as feminist criticism, which theorize and name the practice; and 4. new or at least revised forms of transmission and communication: the anthology and the interdisciplinary conference. While feminist scholarship clearly has not invented either form, it has, I think, transformed the anthology from its function as repository of the old and classical to its current state as a *projection* of the new and innovative. This is, for example, the project of Coppélia Kahn and Gayle Greene's collection, which announces its purchase on the future by the agenda for change embedded in the words of the title, *Making a Difference* (1985). Even an anthology like Elaine Showalter's 1985 collection of essays dating back to 1977 is called *The New Feminist Criticism*. The same claim to project new paradigms could be said to characterize Gilbert and Gubar's editing of the *Norton Anthology of Literature by Women*, also published in 1985. (I know that the latter two volumes are seen by some to participate dangerously in their own sort of canon-making, but I'm going to have to bracket that problem for the time being.)

In addition to these new or transformed objects of study, 1984–85 saw the publication of two works of meta-criticism, overviews and critical accounts of feminist literary activity, Toril Moi's *Sexual/Textual Politics* and K. K. Ruthven's *Feminist Literary Studies*. Coming after the special journal issues devoted to feminist criticism in the 1980s—*Yale French Studies* (1981), *Critical Inquiry* (1981), and *Diacritics* (1982)—these two books, the first by a woman, the second by a man, should make it more embarrassing (but are they ever embarrassed?) for someone now to ask with that annoying combination of exasperation and bewilderment, but what *is* feminist criticism? I do not mean to suggest, of course, that however useful, these books do not present serious epistemological and political problems. On the contrary. But they contribute to the fact that in 1986 one can at least direct one's interlocutor to an answer without running around oneself making photocopies and working up bibliographies. In 1986, then, it has become possible to teach feminist criticism from *books*: real objects that appear on bookstore order lists, and not the eternal handouts and homemade anthologies (though the latter will of necessity continue as the discipline evolves and gets ahead of itself again, and in the interdisciplinary offerings of Women's Studies programs). To simplify, let's say that by normative academic standards, feminist criticism now exists.

So what's the bad news? It hasn't seemed to *make a difference*—at least in the academic institutions I know best, Barnard College and Columbia University. And now I want to tell you three stories about the critical politics of change—the parables announced in my title—that may help us to focus on the current issues in feminist literary scholarship and to think about ways of regrouping for feminism in the 1980s and 1990s.

The stories turn on the problem that feminist criticism has faced—though perhaps not squarely—from the beginning: the relationship between women's writing and the canon. Although feminist thinking, may have radically changed the object of literary study, by *a.* its discovery or recovery of under-read or unknown women writers; and by *b.* its establishment of various traditions of women's writing in England, America, and France, in the standard accounts—textbooks, anthologies, course syllabi—that massive work of recovery and reinterpretation has not received more than token recognition in mainstream curricula. Second, despite the truly groundbreaking work done in feminist criticism, despite the institutional recognition of individual scholars, feminist criticism, however theoretical it may think itself, is not perceived by literary theorists as *theory*. The distinction was made nicely in a recent ad for a position at a major research university which read: "feminist or theorist."

My third point here more specifically addresses the question of the canon. Although there has been major work done on, say, Shakespeare, the *tradition* of "great books" has not been systematically reread from a feminist perspective. Paradoxically, the book that launched feminist criticism, Kate Millett's *Sexual Politics* (1970), has not had the same kind of descendance as, say, Ellen Moers's *Literary Women* (1976). Eve Kosofsky Sedgwick's *Between Men* (1985) on English literature of the mid-eighteenth to the mid-nineteenth centuries, Naomi Schor's *Breaking the Chain* (1985) on the French nineteenth-century novel, and Nancy Vickers's essays on Renaissance writing are a few recent examples and exceptions to the rule. But on the whole, the brokers of the standard curriculum have been left pretty much alone to conduct business as usual. The dominant trend in feminist criticism toward the study of women's writing—theorizing the production and poetics of a female tradition—may at the same time have discouraged theoretical work on the massively male precincts of literary history itself.

In "Treason Our Text: Feminist Challenges to the Literary Canon" (1983), Lillian Robinson argues that we need a "current within feminist criticism that [would go] beyond insistence on representation to consideration of precisely how inclusion of women's writing alters our view of the tradition" (112). And she goes on to ask what I take to be the key question in this third phase of feminist criticism: "Is the canon and hence the syllabus based on it to be regarded as the compendium of excellence or as the record of cultural history?" (We know how most institutions have answered that question.)[2] Finally, she makes the point that there is an important, if generally ignored, difference between the "construction of pantheons, which have no *prescribed* number of places" and the "construction of course syllabi" (112) which do, and which therefore respond to a variety of extra-aesthetic agendas. But I promised parables.

You may know that Columbia College has enjoyed since 1933 a core curriculum which includes a course in the Humanities called "Masterpieces of European Literature and Philosophy," familiarly called "Lit Hum." (I should mention that in a previous incarnation as an assistant professor of French at Columbia, I taught this course for three years.) It will come as no great surprise that a course with such a name has historically included no women writers, even though the second semester (the first semester is the Greeks and Romans) allows for considerable variety since it begins with the Bible, and ends, typically, with Dostoevski. In recent years there have been efforts on the part of the junior faculty and graduate students who teach this course to include the works of women writers. After several failed attempts, this year, presumably because the College is no longer all male, saw a radical change. After much struggle, the principle was admitted that one slot be awarded to a woman writer.

The headline in the January 20, 1986, campus newspaper *Spectator* announced: "Jane Austen now required in spring Lit Hum syllabus." And the opening paragraph reads: "Coeducation will take on a new meaning this spring as Jane Austen's *Pride and Prejudice* becomes the first text by a woman to become required reading for Columbia College's Humanities course." A senior member of the English department, the article goes on to report, is said to have "admitted that some members of the faculty felt that Austen's work was not 'relevant' to the rest of the syllabus, but said her significance as a respected woman author was more important than the work's ability to 'stand up' by itself." There are several thorny issues at stake here: does the presence of women in the classroom require the assignment of a woman writer? If so, on what grounds? If not, on what grounds? Was it okay for the

Humanities course to have continued fifty years without a woman writer, and to continue for the foreseeable future with only one?

In a way, the logic of coeducation—i.e., women as readers—is not really the most fruitful line of argument to take. Not because it isn't defensible, but because it doesn't go far enough. (On the other hand, one must nonetheless make the argument since not to make it authorizes the fiction of a certain hegemony.) To say, for example, that women, Asians, Hispanics, and Blacks, as well as gay men and women—to call up the minorities who are represented and who self-consciously represent themselves as minority voices in the Barnard/Columbia student population—are entitled to study works which reflect "their own historical experiences"[3] does not necessarily make the next point; or rather leaves the premise of the canon-as-course intact. To emphasize minority experience indeed logically implies that the dominant record of experience is also particular, which is to say, historical or historicizable as: European white elite men, generally heterosexual, typically empowered. But it does not address the question of the ways in which this record is rationalized and canonized in the institution, and carved in stone (at Columbia, where the names of the masterpiece writers are inscribed on the library's facade, this is no figure of speech).[4] It also raises in an unexamined manner the question of the relations between literature and reality—or experience. The "reflection" model according to which literature directly mirrors experience is fraught with its own set of theoretical issues, and one has to be prepared to deal with them as well.

I am suggesting that to maintain that "your texts don't speak to our experience" doesn't get at a grittier problem: what is "your" relation to "your" experience? Or, on what grounds does your experience get to pass for the universal, for the transparency of knowledge? As long as that basic deformation is not addressed, the best one will get is the token recognition of a "respected woman author," with everything else left unchanged around it. This is also what allows one's colleagues to assert that *Pride and Prejudice* doesn't have obvious connections to "earlier classical works."[5] And in this sense the choice of an Austen novel could turn out to be a treacherous one. Given Austen's place in the history of the novel, the likelihood is great that students will learn to think of the book (if they do not already have this opinion from their high-school classes) as a masterpiece of the feminine and domestic—the famous "little Bit . . . of Ivory"—as opposed to the more fully human and public literature of the epic, say, or the Russians. The seductive powers of these cultural commonplaces should not be underestimated. Which brings me to my next parable.

When Columbia College finally decided to abandon its position as the last all-male college in the Ivy League (1982), Barnard College decided to work on its image. It undertook a major curriculum review. After a year of meetings, discussion, consultations, etc., a faculty committee proposed the elements of a "core" curriculum. The notion was that students should have a common experience, though not exactly like the monolith of the famous required core taught across the street. In addition to a course in "quantitative reasoning," then, Barnard would offer Freshman Seminars, and try something more individual, more heterogeneous, though to be sure, students would read from the pantheon of "important works" (we were given lists from Columbia and Chicago as guides). Senior, and when they ran out of them, full-time junior faculty members were enlisted, with the help of some outside funding, to develop new inter-disciplinary courses. And to guarantee the interdisciplinarity, the faculty were encouraged to work in groups (or as they came to be called, clusters). A group of us (from Classics, English, Psychology, Russian, Oriental Studies, and Women's Studies) designed and developed what we thought of as a "feminist humanities" syllabus (and the height of political correctness). We would read from the "great works," since that was the collective charge of the program, but we would also read works by women authors, and by writers of color; we would read women's poetry that revises the myths of Penelope and Circe; we would see films and have poetry readings in the original languages; we would read essays from anthropology, psychology, and literary criticism which would offer yet another perspective on these cultural productions of difference, notably of Self and Other.

In the course of a meeting held at the end of the first semester (Fall

Parables and Politics

1984) to review the experience of teaching the seminars, our group presented collectively some thoughts on what we had tried to do in our classes to the larger body of faculty teaching in the program. We all spoke, in different voices (as they say), about different things. Did they want, we asked, to discuss as a body what we all thought now of the general collective project? Did we accept the traditions of the canon? Did we, for instance, have a responsibility to women students as *women* students; to minority students, a growing population at the college? Did we think these were questions to debate? A female philosopher said she couldn't see why or how these were questions that should concern her. A female voice on the side of indifference seemed to authorize the male voices of resentment. A male professor of literature protested that the "charm" of the Freshman Seminar program was its heterogeneity, its diversity; yes, echoed still another voice of protest, we should be idiosyncratic.[6]

What caused the extreme resistance to our appeal to reconsider the canon, the notion of minority and majority culture, the question of female experience? There are of course local ways to explain the episode, but they remain finally beside the point. There is, however, no simple or single explanation of this deep-seated reluctance to change. I have given examples of two quite different sorts. In the Columbia case, the push to require a woman writer would not have succeeded without the liberal guilt generated by new pressures of coeducation. It is not at all clear, moreover, that the presence of Jane Austen on the list means that any movement to transform the curriculum has taken hold. (On the contrary, this is a perfect demonstration of the mainstream recipe: "Add a woman and stir.") In the Barnard story, the collective refusal to admit the principle that women writers should be included in all seminars (on the grounds of fairness and representation: what Robinson calls the "cultural record of history") justified itself on the grounds of "individual" freedom. In both cases the defenders of the status quo resolutely failed to consider as a question the assumptions and effects of their own subjectivity in the construction of syllabi, indeed in the act of reading itself.

The failure to understand that human subjects are not disembodied "eternal values" (as represented in great books), but social, historical, and cultural constructions, is the single greatest obstacle to the transformation of institutional practices that feminist thinking is trying to bring about. More specifically, until those who occupy the majority position, until "men" (which of course often means women, especially, alas, at women's colleges) are willing to question their own relation to the universal; until that happens, the only changes we are going to see in the organization and transmission of knowledge are those we could call "requiring Jane Austen," or the "Jane Austen effect."[7] These gestures are therefore doubly painful to work for (or witness) because they require a simplification of complicated issues—issues about gender and writing and canons—about which "we" do not necessarily agree, in the name of immediate political action or institutional change.

Putting the matter another way, what feminist critical theory thus far has not succeeded in doing is splitting the subject in power from the fascination of his own representation. Can this be done? I grow more and more skeptical.[8]

The gamble was that were we able to produce textual evidence of another subjectivity, what at the beginning of this paper I referred to as the good news (which in another discourse of course is the gospel); were we able to show our specificity, they would perceive their difference; not so much from us, but from their own identity, "differences *within*" (Johnson, *The Critical Difference*, x). But there seems to be little carry over from the women's room to the men's. Thus there is psychoanalysis and feminist psychoanalysis, "*textual theory*" and the practices of Anglo/American feminist criticism (Moi, 86). Recently, for example, a distinguished literary critic who works in the field of psychoanalysis and literature commented on the feminist psychoanalytic project: the problem, he maintained, with the feminist emphasis on mothers and daughters or maternal discourse is that it's "situational": one can't generalize from it; whereas fathers and sons is, well, psychoanalytic because universal(izable).

Another example. I recently visited a mainstreaming program at a large Eastern public university. I spoke with the English literature faculty involved in the project about their efforts to make changes in the basic curricular offerings of the department. Although my charge had been to talk to them about the developments in feminist criticism and theory, much of the discussion turned on material questions: what could one actually teach in the classroom and how? If you add a woman don't you have to subtract a (great) man? How much would it cost in dollars and cents to choose one anthology over another—the Gilbert and Gubar Norton, for instance—and so on. Shortly after my visit, I received a letter from the leader of the workshop that describes the current moment very well, I think:

> I am still a bit puzzled by their response to literary theory. Clearly and understandably their primary concerns are pedagogical, and this was reflected in their questions to you. However, they keep saying that they want more theory even though they have been given a great deal of theory. They have copies of almost all the individual essays in the Showalter collection as well as the major books in the field. How well they have read or understood them, I am not sure. As I prepare for the workshops of the fall semester, I am wondering what approach to take. *Perhaps they do not recognize feminist criticism as theory, or perhaps are looking for a single critical stance rather than the diversity that characterizes feminist criticism.* Do you have any suggestions? (Sara Coulter, January 8, 1985; emphasis mine)

I wish I did. It may well be that it is precisely the "diversity that characterizes feminist criticism" that undermines its effects outside its own sphere of influence. In this sense, little has changed since 1979, when Carolyn Heilbrun, speaking to her colleagues in English departments, observed: "Deconstruction, semiology, Derrida, Foucault may question the very meaning of meaning as we have learned it, but feminism may not do so" ("Spirit," 23). I am torn between thinking it's because we are too apocalyptic, and thinking we haven't been radical enough. And yet, to take just one example, isn't the discovery (Beauvoir's) that femininity is produced by a complex concatenation of discursive and non-discursive events as exciting as the proposition (Foucault's) that sexuality (as it turns out, male) is inseparable from the effects and articulations of power? Or perhaps it is fatal to proceed by comparison: as though a theory that emerged from the collective thinking of feminist scholars could ever impose itself with the effect of the authorial signatures of Freud, Marx, Derrida. In performative terms, I would go further to say that in my experience the perception of authority diminishes in direct proportion to the speaker's proximity to feminist discourse; this is another version of feminist or theorist.

Critical schools or styles, moreover, typically have an institutional base (however metonymic)—the Yale School is the best example of this (for comic relief, see the full-color spread in the *New York Times Magazine*, February 9, 1986); or a dominant figure—De Man, Jameson, Said—who imposes *his* theories through his teaching and the graduate students who work with him. (Figures like these occasionally overcome their difference from each other to share power in, for instance, *The* School of Criticism and Theory—a group not distinguished by its inclusion of notable feminist scholars.) Feminist critics, moreover, have tended to be isolated from each other geographically— the notion that Princeton could hire Elaine Showalter *and* Sandra Gilbert seemed genuinely revolutionary; and even the distinguished individual figures in feminist theory tend to associate themselves with the larger project, demonstrating commonalities rather than insisting upon the uniqueness of their method or position. But if the school model does not seem a promising one for feminist critics, this is not meant to suggest that at work here is a Chorodowian model of affiliation and fluid boundaries between women; or the demonstration of a Gilliganian lack of ego; I'm not even saying I think this is such a great thing; rather I want to emphasize the *effects of institutional realities* in the material elaboration of feminist critical theory.

But you may ask, what has this to do with women's writing and the canon, if I may borrow one of Woolf's famous rhetorical moves in *A Room of One's Own*? And hadn't I announced three parables?

Throughout his overview of feminist literary studies, Ruthven complains about and protests against what he calls "separatist feminism" (13)[9]; what he understands to be an exclusive/exclusionist attention to women's writing. "It would be a pity," he worries, by way of conclusion, if the feminist critique, which has been so successful in identifying andro-centric bias against women writers and in making possible a critical discourse free of such prejudices, should be betrayed by a gynocritics developed along separatist lines. For that would simply reproduce the polarity between women's writing and men's which feminist criticism set out to combat in the first place. And it would also make it that much harder next time to persuade men and women that they have far too much to learn from one another to risk going their separate ways (128).

Since I myself have been dubbed a "partisan of separatist criticism" (Munich, 255), I would like to suggest here a more accurate and useful way to think about women's writing. I would argue that it is precisely through the processes of recovery, revision, and "revisionary reread-ing" (Kolodny, "A Map," 59) which constitute the characteristic ges-tures of the work of women's writing that we can learn how to chal-lenge the false continuities (origins and influences) of the canon: a collection of texts that might more truthfully be designated as "men's writing."

In many ways the reconstruction of feminism, like deconstruction which involves two principles or steps, is a doubled dealing: "a *reversal* of the classical opposition *and* a general *displacement* of the system."[10] But the reconstruction sought by feminist literary theory necessarily operates a specific inflection (and displacement) of that set of gestures: the establishment of a female tradition—a move that by its own claims to representation seeks to unsettle the claims of literary history—*and* a steady, Medusa-like gaze from its own genealogies at a tradition that has never thought to think back through its mothers. Put another way, my argument here is that a feminist look at the canon (the system) will reveal the petrification of the gender hierarchies that regulate the institutionalization of literature, and displace the asymmetries those hierarchies install. Contrary to what Ruthven imagines, then, I would argue that by its attention to the questions of feminist literary theory—who reads, who writes, whose interests are served by this reading and writing?— the study of women's writing *returns* separatism from the margins to the nervous "I" of the dominant beholders. And in my view,

67

meaningful change within the institution will come only from this return to sender that dislocates the universal subject from his place at the center of the dominant discourse.

The third parable. In the literature of female signature there is a text, a long novel, though that term domesticates the work's explosion of generic restraints (or rather a kind of Bakhtinian heteroglossia reigns instead), that takes up the question of the pantheon, the canon, and the place in it for the woman writer. The work is Germaine de Staël's *Corinne, or Italy* (1807). Corinne, the heroine, begins the tour of Rome she has designed to capture the imagination of Oswald, the melancholy Englishman who has come to Italy to recover his health, and recover from the grief brought on by the death of his father.

Corinne, a poet and improviser whose crowning on the steps of the Capitol dramatically introduces the lovers to each other, takes Oswald first to the Pantheon where one can see "the busts of the most famous artists: they decorate the niches where the gods of the ancients had been placed." Corinne explains that her deepest desire is to have her place there as well: "I've already chosen mine, she said, showing him an empty niche." If we ask again, "how does the inclusion of women's writing alter our view of the tradition," *Corinne* offers an exemplary set of answers: it rereads Greek myth through Roman architecture; it incarnates cultural relativism; it articulates the history of Classicism and Romanticism; it politicizes, by making it a question of public display, the notion of genius; it stages the problem of subjectivity; and dramatizes the question of the artist's relation to the social. The novel had enormous impact on (women) writers in France, England, and America. Need I add that it belongs neither to the canon of the French novel (though because of de Staël's status as an intellectual and the author of *On Germany* the book gets honorable mention) nor to the pantheon of world literature. In other words, the niche still remains empty.

When Corinne realizes she is about to die (young), and is too ill to perform, she has her verses read, in a final theatrical event, by a young girl. She also arranges before her death to have her tiny niece, Juliette (the daughter of Oswald and Corinne's English half-sister Lucille), learn to speak Italian and play the harp: just like Corinne, but of course with the difference a generation makes. Thus the artist in her lifetime arranges for and underwrites her legacy: what I will call a feminist "aftertext" (Berg, 219).

Barthes, we know, has argued that the Death of the Author is coterminous with, if not brought about by, the Birth of the Reader. Although he records the former event with a jubilation feminist critics will not all necessarily share, there is, perhaps, good reason to appropriate and revise the paradigm. For this is our only hope. Confronted with the persistence of the empty niche, it becomes our task to stage the possibility of a different sort of continuity. Not the biological and murderous simplicity that appeals so much to the father and son teams of our cultural paradigms (à la Harold Bloom after Sigmund Freud), but a more complex legacy that like Corinne's passes on its values in life to another generation through reading and its performatives; and like Lucy Snowe, it authorizes its passions from another and finally ambiguous scene of writing.

Legacies have everything to do with the future of feminism.

P.S. Two months after the writing of this paper, the staff at Columbia involved in teaching the Humanities course voted (with an extremely narrow margin) to make other changes in the syllabus. Included in the fall semester (the Greeks and the Romans) now are Sappho's poetry and the Homeric Hymn to Demeter. In the spring, Rabelais has been dropped to be replaced by Boccaccio, and *The Princess of Clèves* has been added. The political determinants of these and other revisions are not clearly feminist in impulse or agenda, but it does seem fair to conclude that paradoxically without the "Jane Austen effect" nothing would have changed at all. Since the voted-in list also featured one optional slot, who can say where it will end.

NOTES

I would like to thank Christina Crosby and the Women's Studies Steering Committee for creating the panel, and the students at Wesleyan for being such a good audience.

Getting Personal

I also read "Parables and Politics" at a faculty seminar on feminist criticism at UCLA in April 1986. The other panelists were Naomi Schor and Anne Mellor. I thank Sara Melzer and Anne Mellor for including me in that occasion.

1. The 1985 talk at the Pembroke Center has been published under the title "Changing the Subject" in both *Coming to Terms* (the volume of essays emerging from the occasion, edited by Elizabeth Weed) and in *Feminist Studies/Critical Studies* (edited by Teresa de Lauretis); as well as in my *Subject to Change*.

2. In Denis Donoghue's 1986 "A Criticism of One's Own," further subtitled "Feminism's Agenda in Literary Studies," Robinson's discussion is cited *against* feminist critics—notably Gilbert and Gubar in their anthology, and Elaine Showalter in hers—who, the claim goes, operate (select texts) according to "political and sociological" criteria and not questions of "literary merit" (147). When the argument is made for merit, Donoghue finds it "desperate": "We are to believe that literary criteria are incorrigibly man-made values, and are compromised by the power they enforce" (149–50). I review his position in "Man on Feminism."

3. Marcellus Blount, now assistant professor in the Columbia English department, quoted in *Spectator*. Blount was erroneously described then as "lecturer in the Afro-American Literature Department" which did not exist in 1986. He is currently director of the recently created African-American Studies program.

4. In the fall of 1989, the *New York Times* published a photo of the library wall upon which one can read the names Plato, Aristotle, Demosthenes, Cicero, etc., graced by a one hundred and forty foot-long banner "bearing the names of great female authors": Pizan, Sor Juana, Brontë, Dickinson, Woolf, etc. According to the account, the banner was the work of Laura Hotchkis Brown. In the "Notes & Comments" section of the *New Criterion*, this "radical initiative" does not go unnoticed: "The names that adorned Brown's banner are interesting, of course, as an example of what happens when the study of literature becomes radically ideologized. For what is striking about the majority of these names is that they are minor, if not indeed, marginal, figures" (3).

5. I am grateful to Susan Winnett, who thinks interestingly about these questions, for her details about the Columbia discussion. Another footnote to this discussion is the rejection for the woman writer's slot of *The Princess of Clèves*, a novel of perfectly classical origins, a masterpiece of the French canon, and that has also been the subject of a fair amount of feminist criticism over the past few years. This novel, which builds clearly on the French tradition of reflection on the "human condition," was rejected as a candidate for the woman writer's slot on the grounds that it was too "slight." But this was not the only obstacle to inclusion. In the course of one of the meetings, a specific criticism was leveled at the opening section of the novel, the description of the court of Henry II, as being too difficult. Finally, a senior male colleague is reported to have remarked that "the husband is the only interesting character in the novel." That, at least, is an imaginative line of resistance.

6. The seminars were grouped together in large thematic categories: "Literary Reflections on the Human Condition," "The Individual and the Social Order," "Aspects

of the Modern Tradition." To suggest the flavor of the enterprise I have selected the blurb for "Literary Reflections on the Human Condition": "Each of these seminars focuses on an enduring or timeless genre through a close reading of texts drawn from the sweep of classical and modern literature." In the common reading list—there were of course individual variations—for the courses collected under these headings no (or one) woman writer appeared on the syllabus.

7. I owe the phrase "requiring Jane Austen," to Rachel Brownstein, and "the Jane Austen effect" to Ruth Yeazell (in discussion at a faculty seminar at UCLA).

8. In conversation after the talk at Wesleyan, Laura Wechsler pointed out that I offer too sanguine a view of institutions by suggesting that the subject in power's relation to the representation of his own power is somehow unwitting (a blind spot that would disappear with corrected vision), and not chosen and assumed. The remark reminded me of an exchange with the Dean of Columbia College who argued that *a.* if there were not canonical answers, there were canonical questions; and that *b.* the required courses were indeed about the powerful, and I was talking about the powerless. It's true that it is less easy to come back from the equanimous assertion of hegemonic values.

And if we ever imagined that outside the rigid restraints of academic life things were more fluid, the recent Congress at PEN made MLA look like Brigadoon. No president of MLA, at least in recent years, would dare to assert publicly, as Mailer did: "If there are not enough women who would be suited to those panels, why put them on? All we'd be doing is lowering the level of discussion . . . . We didn't want a Congress that would establish a political point at the cost of considerable mediocrity" (*Village Voice*, January 26, 1986; 54–55). Whether a meeting of PEN that doesn't find women, except for Susan Sontag, "intellectual enough"; a faculty group who find *The Princess of Clèves* too "slight"; a departmental search that can't find a female star who would shine brightly enough in their firmament: these questions return inevitably to the relation of subjectivity and knowledge and the power relations that articulate it.

9. In *Reading Woman* Mary Jacobus performs an astute analysis of Ruthven's obsession with separatism: his "own discourse on feminist criticism," she writes, "retains its imaginary mastery of the discourse of feminism. The measure is separation (feminist criticism as castration) or a reassuring image of wholeness (feminist criticism as the imaginary, narcissistic completion of critical lack): the phallic woman, in short, has something to offer the institution of criticism after all" (285).

10. The argument continues: "It is on that condition alone that deconstruction will provide the means of *intervening* in the field of oppositions it criticizes and which is also a field of non-discursive forces" (Derrida, *Marges*, 392; in Culler, 85–86). Whether the operations of displacement actually effect an intervention in the scene of non-discursive structures, in the hierarchies of university life, for example, is to my mind the great question of deconstructive criticism as a politics.

6

Dreaming, Dancing, and the Changing Locations of Feminist Criticism, 1988

This essay belongs in its origins to more than one occasion: the conference "Feminism and the Dream of a Plural Culture" (Queens College) and the colloquium at the School of Criticism and Theory (Dartmouth College), both held in 1988. In its final revised form here, however, the essay reflects my effort to make the problems of a North American criticism meaningful (less local) to a European audience at two subsequent destinations: the first in Paris at a conference on "Cultural Translation" (November 1988); the second, for a new graduate program in Women's Studies at the University of Utrecht (November 1988).

I see the attempt to produce a translation within feminism between cultural contexts and languages as part of a more general endeavor— for critical practice in the '90s—to resist the distinction cultural studies/ feminist studies that has already come to fashion itself on the exclusionary model I describe in "Parables and Politics": feminist or theorist. In my view, feminist criticism, through its emphasis on the cultural and social narratives of gender, belongs at the heart of the cultural studies project.[1]

At "Feminism and the Dream of a Plural Culture," I was to be the "literature person" on a panel called "Gender, Race, Culture: Theoretical Implications." (My copanelists were sociologist Barbara Omolade, and anthropologist Brackette Williams.) I wasn't sure I was really ready to take this on. I had been trying in my seminars over the last several years to work through the implications for feminist literary theory of rezoning critical strategies at the intersections of gender, race,

Dreaming, Dancing

and culture. But despite the work, I had found myself repeatedly confronted by certain knots that I was reluctant to untie in public. Nonetheless, in a gesture of collegiality, I decided to run the risk of premature exposure; the structure of the talk that resulted, originally called "Whose Dream?" bears the mark of that uncertainty and ambivalence.

At the School of Criticism and Theory the colloquium was the occasion at which each seminar teacher's work was discussed in a public forum. The work (an essay, a chapter, a book in progress) was circulated to the community—seminar participants (one's own students), other faculty (their students), etc.—before being discussed by the group at large. The discussion normally followed a formal critique by the Director of the School and the faculty member's response to it. The other faculty teaching seminars that summer were Mary Ann Caws, Thomas Greene, and Edward Said.

I am to speak these words in Europe, but I have been searching for them in the United States of America. A few years ago I would have spoken of the common oppression of women, the gathering movement of women around the globe, the hidden history of women's resistance and bonding, the failure of all previous politics to recognize the universal shadow of patriarchy, the belief that women now, in a time of rising consciousness and global emergency, may join across all national and cultural boundaries to create a society free of domination, in which "sexuality, politics, . . . work, . . . intimacy . . . thinking itself will be transformed." I would have spoken these words as a feminist who "happened" to be a white United States citizen, conscious of my government's proven capacity for violence and arrogance of power, but as self-separated from that government, quoting without second thought Virginia Woolf's statement in *Three Guineas* that "as a woman I have no country. As a woman I want no country. As a woman my country is the whole world." That is not what I come here to say in 1984 (Adrienne Rich, *Blood, Bread, and Poetry,* 210–11).

These words written in the United States to be spoken in Europe come from the opening paragraphs of Rich's essay, "Notes Toward a Politics of Location" (a talk originally given at the First Summer School of Critical Semiotics, Conference on Women, Feminist Identity and

73

Society in the 1980s, at Utrecht). For Rich, location begins with the "geography closest in—the body," particularized: "a North American Jew, born and raised three thousand miles from the war in Europe"; "whiteness as a point of location for which I need to take responsibility." *She concludes her prelude to the discussion of these politics with a final remark about her mode of enunciation:* "I come here with notes but without absolute conclusions. This is not a sign of loss of faith or hope. These notes are the marks of a struggle to keep moving, a struggle for accountability" (211).

The choice to have the essay take the form of notes characterizes a mode of theorization and self-inscription that I call a "poetics of location." In this shift of emphasis from an account of a feminist struggle in the world to an attention to the struggle as a resistance in form, I also produce a translation from Rich's activist positionality as a "radical feminist" to the less glamorous and much maligned posture of my own, an academic "bourgeois feminist." From within the university—where she is also some of the time—I read Rich reading the world. In a way, my paper is an embodiment of that double move; it is also about the extreme difficulty of continuing thus located.

This is the agenda of the conference, "Feminism and the Dream of a Plural Culture," held at Queens College in February 1988.

The conference pursues the inter-implications of gender, race and culture, starting from positions within feminism; it explores the ways feminism brings new kinds of thinking to bear on culture. From a feminist politics of acknowledgment of difference and struggle against hierarchy, and a notion of race and culture as poles of positive identity, what relations are possible cross-culturally and inter-racially? This question assumes special urgency at a city college whose diverse students and faculty need a vocabulary for thinking and talking about their differences.

As I began to write this essay, the impasse in feminism over the issues delineated above dominated the rhetorical horizon. It was clear that feminist theory had arrived at a crisis in language, a crisis notably inseparable from the pronouns of subjectivity: between the indictment of the feminist universal as a white fiction brought by women of color

74

Dreaming, Dancing

and the poststructuralist suspicion of a grounded subject, what are the conditions under which as feminists one (not to say "I") can say "we"? On what grounds could one locate political agency for feminist subjects? This is the specific knot of the dilemma that in the United States has come to be referred to as "identity politics."[2] *The conflict may also be sketched here schematically as a matter of positioning in language between two asymmetrically posed figures. Imagine on the one hand the deconstructionist figuration of a female (reading) subject (one tends in these discussions to take the reader for the human subject) reading "as a woman"—her identity permanently deferred in the gap between her existence and the figure of woman. And on the other, bodily facing this "as a woman" woman Sojourner Truth asking her famous rhetorical question "Ain't I a woman?"; the phrase, uttered as a declaration of rights, of entitlement, for a woman of color, a black woman, also to be a woman. This captures, I think, but at the same time of course deceptively reduces the multiplicity of the actual positionings within the boundaries of that map.*[3]

In what follows, I try to give a sense of the complexities of the territory; to ask, given those complexities, what kinds of discursive and, more poignantly, personal modes of relation can come to exist between women (and men) in feminism? What follows is a montage of quotations that seemed to offer a way of bringing together voices that don't normally address each other. We could also think of this juxtaposition as an exercise in feminist intertextualities; a process of reading through, rather than towards, that Mary Jacobus describes in Reading Woman *as "correspondences": its "itinerary incomplete and . . . destination deferred" (292); a choreography of bodies on the move, sometimes in synch, more often, in collision.*[4] *I have chosen to italicize my own discourse rather than the quotations in order to emphasize and mark the shift of attention to the quotations themselves.*

In "A Manifesto for Cyborgs: Science, Technology, and Socialist Feminism in the 1980s," Donna Haraway, at an angle to Rich, also addresses these issues at length (the passage below follows an opening discussion entitled "An Ironic Dream of a Common Language for

75

Women in the Integrated Circuit"; it appears under the segment "Fractured Identities."

It has become difficult to name one's feminism by a single adjective—or even to insist in every circumstance upon the noun. Consciousness of exclusion through naming is acute. Identities seem contradictory, partial, and strategic. With the hard-won recognition of their social and historical constitution, gender, race, and class cannot provide the basis for belief in "essential" unity. There is nothing about being "female" that naturally binds women . . . . And who counts as "us" in my own rhetoric? Which identities are available to ground such a potent political myth called "us," and what could motivate enlistment in this collectivity? Painful fragmentation among feminists (not to mention among women) along every possible fault line has made the concept of *woman* elusive, an excuse for the matrix of women's dominations of each other. For me—and for many who share a similar historical location in white, professional middle class, female, radical, North American, mid-adult bodies—the sources of a crisis in political identity are legion. The recent history for much of the U.S. left and U.S. feminism has been a response to this kind of crisis by endless splitting and searches for a new essential unity. But there has also been a growing recognition of another response through coalition—affinity, not identity (179–80).

The use of quotation in "Whose Dream?" was meant both to foreground the social plural of dreaming analyzed by Rich and Haraway and to destabilize my own position in relation to that project. My own dream does not appear here, but it was of course the invitation to dream, to think about dreams that lured me into the writing in the first place. Dream passages from seminar readings pressed themselves forward; the shape of the paper rapidly took form from the quotations which seemed to lead to each other, against each other, without me. I say this not to trivialize the politics entailed in an aesthetics of juxtaposition, but rather to signal the ways in which questions of theory are bound up with the material spread of language: in the themes of dreams and nightmares, bridges and dances; in the interstices of silence and conflict (this is something like Pina Bausch meets feminist theory.)[5]

Dreaming, Dancing

I. Whose Dream?

*To begin, the enigmatic prose of the opening paragraphs to Zora
Neale Hurston's 1937 novel,* Their Eyes Were Watching God.

*I've chosen Hurston's novel in part because it has been a precursor
text for many contemporary black women writers, who have played a
powerful role in framing feminist debate, but also because Hurston,
who studied cultural anthropology—pursuing the question of black
identity ethnographically—was self-consciously involved in performing the work of cultural translation:*

Ships at a distance have every man's wish on board. For some they come
in with the tide. For others they sail forever on the horizon, never out of
sight, never landing until the Watcher turns his eyes away in resignation,
his dreams mocked to death by Time. That is the life of men.

Now, women forget all those things they don't want to remember, and
remember everything they don't want to forget. The dream is the truth.
Then they act and do things accordingly (9).

*These lines are prologue to the narrative of a woman, a black woman,
Janie Crawford, who comes back "from burying the dead," in particular from burying Tea Cake, the man with whom she lived a dream, to
tell her story to her best friend Pheoby. I leave these lines in place as
a framing puzzle to the reflection of this paper.*

*For now I want Hurston's parable to ask the question behind my
title: "Whose Dream?" Does it matter who dreams (or writes) the
dream of Life, of Time? Man or woman? White man or black woman?
Black man or black woman? Straight woman or lesbian woman? What
will the gender of the dreamer, the race of the dreamer, tell us about
the dream? What gets left out of Black and White, Black or White?
What is the relation of difference to plural? Sexism to Racism? Feminism to Racism? Race to Theory?*

*These are too many questions to try to answer. As Hurston's narrator
says later in the novel, "There are years that ask questions and years
that answer." I think we must see these years of the eighties as years*

77

that ask questions. But what seems clear enough is that after two decades of what is referred to in the United States as the second wave of feminism, it has become impossible, however belatedly that impossibility is understood, to continue theorizing as if the question of gender, the pronouns and articles of women's identity under patriarchy, of sexual difference in culture and society, could be feminism's only question; as if there were a single, unitary subject of feminism. As Rich, thinking back over our, her own, recent history of the feminist project writes in "Notes Toward a Politics of Location,"

> some of us, calling ourselves radical feminists, never meant anything less by women's liberation than the creation of a society without domination; we never meant less than the making new of all relationships. The problem was that we did not know whom we meant when we said "we" (217).

Or as Hazel Carby puts it pointedly in "White Woman Listen! Black Feminism and the Boundaries of Sisterhood": "In other words, of white feminists we must ask, what exactly do you mean when you say 'WE'??" *(233).*

In this sense, we could say, that the time has come for "white women" (which of course is not one woman either) to interrogate the language of feminism, to make more complicated demands on feminist theory and practice, resisting self-consciously the twin trap of either "desexualizing" gender, making it, as Teresa de Lauretis puts it, "merely a metaphor, a question of différance, of purely discursive effects," *or* "androgynizing it (claiming the same experience of material conditions for both genders in a given class, race or culture)" *(Technologies of Gender, II). For now this resistance will take the form of an acute attention to the language of identity as it inheres in the acts of enunciation and address: speaking as a ("as a"—fill in the blank), to whom, from where, for whom?*

I. THE PLURAL OF DECONSTRUCTION

Against the gendered dreaming of Hurston's text, I want to juxtapose Jacques Derrida's degendered dream, recalled aloud, so to speak, in a written interview that Christie McDonald conducted with him for the

78

journal Diacritics *in 1981, an issue devoted to feminist criticism. The interview is called "Choreographies," and the passage in which the dream occurs comes as Derrida's reply to McDonald's last question:* "What are our chances of 'thinking *difference*' not so much before sexual difference, as you say, as taking off 'from' it? What would you say is our chance and 'who' are we sexually?" (75). Derrida answers:

> what if we were to reach, what if we were to approach here . . . the area of a relationship to the other where the code of sexual marks would no longer be discriminating? The relationship would not be a-sexual, far from it, but would be sexual otherwise: beyond the binary difference that governs the decorum of all codes, beyond the opposition feminine/masculine, beyond bisexuality as well, beyond homosexuality and heterosexuality which come to the same thing. As I dream of saving the chance that this question offers I would like to believe in the multiplicity of sexually marked voices. . . . Where would the "dream" of the innumerable come from, if it is indeed a dream? Does the dream itself not prove that what is dreamt of must be there in order for it to provide the dream? Then too, I ask you, what kind of dance would there be, or would there be one at all, if the sexes were not exchanged according to rhythms that vary considerably? (76).

I have been struck by the seductive power this dream seems to hold; specifically, given the unabashed hetero- (not to say phallogo-) centrism of its tone, by the "citational" privilege it enjoys in a variety of feminist discussions. Susan Suleiman, for instance, in her essay on the "politics and poetics of female eroticism" glosses approvingly Derrida's dream as the text of a desire to move past the number two, in order to get to her own account of stories by women writers that rewrite the body. The dream, Suleiman comments is

> to get beyond not only the number one—the number that determines unity, of body or of self—but also beyond the number *two*, which determines difference, antagonism, and exchange conceived of as merely the coming together of opposites. That this dream is perhaps impossible is suggested. Its power remains, however, because the desire it embodies is a desire for both endless complication and creative movement (24).

This semiotic reading of "eternal complication" takes her to a dance "between persons of undecidable gender" choreographed by Hélène

Cixous. In this case, it is a "French Feminist" who spins out the metaphorical implications of the trope of an indifferent, undifferentiating plural:

> And then if I spoke about a person whom I met and who shook me up, herself being moved and I moved to see her moved, and she, feeling me moved, being moved in turn, and whether this person is a she [*un elle*] and a he [*une il*] and a he [*une il*] and a she [*un elle*] and a shehe [*une ellil*] and a heshe [*une ilelle*], I want to be able not to lie, I don't want to stop her if she trances, I want him, I want her, I will follow her (Cixous, in Suleiman, 24).

Suleiman is one of several literary critics to have enlisted the philosopher's dream in a feminist analysis; most symptomatically, perhaps, Toril Moi, in Sexual/Textual Politics, *turns to Derrida as a visionary of the future. Moi describes her book as an introduction to feminist literary theory as practiced in the United States and in France. As she concludes her final chapter, "Marginality and Subversion" (which turns around the work of Julia Kristeva), she moves from her translation of Kristeva's vision of language ("as opened up to the free play of the signifier") "into" feminism, and the subject (in process), to the Derrida of "Choreographies." She characterizes the dream as "sybilline and suggestive," as befits a "utopian utterance" (172), and then leaves it in its oracular location without further comment, giving Derrida's dream literally the last word.*

To be sure, for a feminism focused on the question of sexual difference and difference in language, the dream of the innumerable figures a dance of playful possibility. And why shouldn't feminists have fun? But at the same time, it is, I think, the exclusive emphasis in deconstructive and feminist rhetorics on a radically decontextualized sexual difference that has papered over—with extremely serious consequences—both the institutional and political differences between men and women and the equally powerful social and cultural differences between women.

In the first case—the institutional and political differences between men and women—one might simply ask: But who here is dancing? Who leading the dance?

Dreaming, Dancing

Cherríe Moraga writes in "The Slow Dance,"

And I move women around the floor, too—women I think enamored with me. My mother's words rising up from inside me—"A *real* man, when he dances with you, you'll know he's a *real* man by how he holds you in the back." I think, *yes*, someone who can guide you around a dance floor and so, I do. Moving these women kindly, surely, even superior. *I can handle these women.* They want this. And I do too. (423)

In "Any Theory of the 'Subject' Has Always Been Appropriated by the 'Masculine,' " a chapter from Luce Irigaray's 1974 Speculum of the Other Woman—which deals at great length with Freud's discourse on femininity in several chapters called "The Blind Spot of an Old Dream of Symmetry"—Irigaray writes (deconstructing, one might say, Derrida's dream in advance):

The "subject" henceforth will be multiple, plural, sometimes di-formed, but it will still postulate itself as the cause of all the mirages that can be enumerated endlessly and therefore put back together as one. A fantastic, phantasmatic fragmentation. A destruc(tura)tion in which the "subject" is shattered, scuttled, while still claiming surreptitiously that he is the reason for it all.... The "subject" plays at multiplying himself, even deforming himself, in this process. . . . He is masculine and feminine and the relationships between them (135–36).

In other words, following Irigaray, the dream of the innumerable dreamt from within the dream of philosophy's turning in on itself—turning itself inside out—seems only to come out to two sides of the same coin. When the philosopher is interviewed by the feminist and left in the position of the truth, could the dream escape his truth? Do the discursive positionings of the interview structure necessarily keep the dominant subject in place?

Despite the plural of "choreographies," do we not have here in the "othering" of feminism as a body scrutinized and judged yet another instance of what Hortense Spillers has called the "exquisite dance of textual priorities" that conceals on the part of "patriarchists" and white feminists alike, its own investments in the powers of domination? (79) Or, as Naomi Schor wonders in an essay on poststructuralism and feminism called "Dreaming Dissymmetry": "At the risk of being a wallflower at the carnival of plural sexualities, I would ask: what is it to say that the discourse of pure indifference/pure difference is not the last or (less triumphantly) the latest ruse of phallocentrism?" *(109).*

But there are of course other problems with this dance, besides not getting asked. As I said earlier, what the rhetoric of an unlocatable plural masks—in the "area of its relation to the other"—are the claims precisely of other locational identities, the intersection of multiple modes of acting in the world that as feminists "we" must now find ways to address, recognizing the so-called other as subject.

2. "DANCING THROUGH THE MINEFIELD," OR, FURTHER PERILS OF SOCIAL DANCING

In "Dancing Through the Minefield," an essay on the theory, practice, and politics of feminist literary criticism, first published in the journal Feminist Studies *in 1980 and since anthologized in Elaine Showalter's* The New Feminist Criticism *(1985)—which makes it now a feminist "classic"—Annette Kolodny, reviewing the decade of criticism that preceded her essay, remarks that feminist critics, despite the remarkable accomplishments of their work, have not been* "welcomed onto the train," *but rather* "forced to negotiate a minefield" *(149).* "The very energy and diversity of our enterprise," *she writes,* "have rendered us vulnerable to attack on the grounds that we lack both definition and coherence" *(149). This* "apparent disarray," *she claims, should place feminist critics* "securely where, all along, we should have been: camped out, on the far side of the minefield, with the other pluralists and pluralisms" *(159). Pluralism, she goes on to argue,* "informs feminist literary inquiry not simply as a description of what already exists but, more importantly, as the only critical stance consistent with the current status of the larger women's movement" *(162). Her final remarks return to the dangers of dancing:*

> In my view, it is a fine thing for many of us, individually, to have traversed the minefield; but that happy circumstance will only prove of lasting importance if, together, we expose it for what it is (the male fear of sharing

power and significance with women) and deactivate its components, so that others, after us, may literally dance through the minefield (163).

In 1982, Feminist Studies published thirty-five pages of replies to Kolodny's piece. The bulk of the replies were written by two feminist critics, Elly Bulkin and Rena Grasso Patterson; both address, with differing emphases, but equal indignation, what they take to be the classism, heterosexism, and racism of Kolodny's essay. Notably, Kolodny's notions of "pluralism" and "diversity" come under attack for their insufficient attention to:

> *real and consequential* differences of race, class, and sexual identification [which] often entail the destructive impact among women of unequal and oppressive power relations, their history, and their continuation into the present. To gloss them over with a contentless concept of "diversity" falsifies and perpetuates the social and economic differences separating women (659–60).

Outside the pages of Feminist Studies, *Kolodny's pluralism was also generally seen negatively as a positioning that by* "refusing to judge, conceals and preserves the white male hegemony of the critical establishment" *(Meese, 142); and that, as Jane Marcus puts the matter in* "Storming the Toolshed," "minimizes the differences within feminist criticism, obscuring the theoretical and practical differences between 'insiders'—'academic' feminist critics—and 'outsiders'—black, Marxist, and lesbian feminists working outside the academy" *(Marcus, 217– 18).* "Pluralism," *Gayatri Spivak argues,* "is the method employed by the *central* authorities to neutralize opposition by seeming to accept it. The gesture of pluralism on the part of the *marginal* can only mean capitulation to the center" *(in Marcus, 218).* "Dancing shoes," *Marcus concludes,* "will not do. We still need our heavy boots and mine detectors" *(218).*

As we have seen, both the critical plural of a mainstream, white woman's feminism, and a "degendered" poststructuralist "multiplicity of sexually marked voices" can be seen to erase the bodies of differentiated social subjects. The one imposes a false feminist universal that seems to be complicitous with a central institutional authority; the other reveals itself to be the cover for a phallocentric subject who measures difference by himself. What then might be the feminist dream of a plural culture? What language would be adequate to represent "real and consequential differences"?

At the conference at Queens College, Bell Hooks remarked: "We already live in a plural culture, but it is a plural lived under domination—what copanelist Barbara Omolade called the 'racial patriarchy'—the dream is of a plural culture under liberation."

3. "OTHER DREAMS, OTHER DANCES"

I want to place in epigraph here a passage from Cherríe Moraga's preface to This Bridge Called My Back, *an anthology of writings by self-identified "radical women of color." Moraga writes:*

> Literally, for two years now, I have dreamed of a bridge. In writing this conclusion, I fight the myriad voices that live inside me. The myriad voices that stop my pen at every turn of the page. They are the voices that tell me here I should be talking more "materialistically" about the oppression of women of color, that I should be plotting out a "strategy" for Third World Revolution. But what I really want to write about is faith.

And she concludes, before signing: "In the dream, I am always met at the river" *(xviii–xix).*

At the end of her much anthologized 1977 essay "Toward a Black Feminist Criticism" (which now appears in the same volume of feminist criticism as Kolodny's), Barbara Smith turns to the politics of dreams as she seeks a ground for closure.

> What I want this essay to do is lead everyone who reads it to examine *everything* that they have ever thought and believed about feminist culture and to ask themselves how their thoughts connect to the reality of Black women's writing and lives. I want to encourage in white women, as a first step, a sane accountability to all the women who write and live on this soil. I want most of all for Black women and Black lesbians somehow not to be so alone. This last will require the most expansive of revolutions as well as many new words to tell us how to make this revolution real. I finally want to express how much easier both my waking and my sleeping

hours would be if there were one book in existence that would tell me something specific about my life. One book based in Black feminist and Black lesbian experience, fiction or nonfiction. Just work to reflect the reality that I and the Black women whom I love are trying to create. When such a book exists then each of us will not only know better how to live, but how to dream (183–84).

Like the rhetoric of Martin Luther King's famous dream of brother-hood, Smith's manifesto of sisterhood embodies the faith of performative dreaming.

But Smith is also talking about something else.[6] Smith's revolution that would make the dream reality and in turn make possible other dreams about, perhaps, other realities, requires texts: an imagination of the dream in writing. (It's been said, for instance, that Audre Lorde wrote her autobiography Zami *for Barbara Smith, to prove that one could be a black lesbian feminist and survive, joyfully.)*

Like much of the early prescriptive feminist literary criticism calling for literary role models and positive identities, Smith's discourse of authenticity may seem old-fashioned. In the moment of Theory in which "we" live, Smith's passionate belief in origin, stable meaning, and the adequacy of the sign to account for the thing it represents, stands out in bold and archaic relief against the poststructuralist land-scape. This is both its strength and its weakness.[7]

The invocation of a lived reality as a shaping and material constraint upon textuality is finally the single most serious—and unanswered— critique to be brought against a deconstructionist requirement of lin-guistic self-reflexivity. Yet at the same time, Hazel Carby argues, Smith's "reliance on a common, or shared, experience" *between* "black women as critics and black women as writers who represent black women's reality" *results in a theoretical positioning open to charges of essentialism and ahistoricism* (Reconstructing Womanhood, 16). *Put another way, if talking about women as though all women were white excludes women of color from the definition of women, other erasures of difference are produced by assuming, as Carby points out, a* "simple one-to-one correspondence between fiction and reality" *(9).*

Smith's dream takes as its truth a grounded politics of identity. Thus, though it is a dream that struggles against the inequities that inhere in the power of the figure two—the figure, as Irigaray has shown, that always returns to the dominion of the one: "the movement to speak of the 'other' in a language already systematized by/for the same" *(139)—it is not in its language a dream of the innumerable.*

The dominated have learned to count their numbers; that numbers count.

Earlier in this discussion I said that I would be raising some questions about feminism and racism, racism and deconstruction, deconstruction and feminism. I want to turn now, as I move toward a conclusion, to an essay that in many ways, though not all, gets quickly to the heart of these questions in its title. This is Barbara Christian's "The Race for Theory." Christian, arguing first against an academically hegemonic move by theory to take over the literary world, questions the "color" of theory: "People of color have always theorized," *she writes;* "our theorizing . . . is often in narrative forms. . . . My folk, in other words, have always been a race of theory—though more in the form of the hieroglyph, a written figure which is both sensual and abstract, both beautiful and communicative" *(226).*

Like Smith, Christian sees literature as a matter of personal survival, and criticism as a reading that will help ensure that the literature she reads will have "continuity and survive" *for others. For the conclusion of her essay, she turns to Audre Lorde's "Poetry Is Not a Luxury," for her last word:*

> Right now, I could name at least ten ideas I would have found intolerable or incomprehensible and frightening, except as they came after dreams and poems. This is not idle fantasy . . . . We can train ourselves to respect our feelings and to transpose them into a language so they can be shared. And where that language does not yet exist, it is our poetry which helps to fashion it. Poetry is not only dream and vision; it is the skeleton architecture of our lives. It lays the foundations for a future of change, a bridge across our fears of what has never been before (236).

You will have noticed that in most of the instances in which I have quoted a dream passage, the dream comes toward the end of the essay in which it appears. The dreams tend to occur in a writer's text

*as a way of pointing to an as yet unrealized program of social change;
their occurrence in the place of closure, as a move toward closure,
engages and exhorts the reader to share the dream, to imagine and help
create a world, a text, a mode of being in the world beyond what has
already been imagined and realized. This move is not surprising—in
fact it is almost predictable—since most of the pieces I have been
working with articulate social and cultural agendas animated by utopian impulses: social critical theory that in the face of historically
unsatisfactory reality looks for an elsewhere in which to locate the
vision of an otherwise. The dreams arise so frequently in this discourse,
I think, because of the radical difficulty inhabiting the feminist project
of bringing about social changes that touch on fundamental notions
of human identity.*

*These then are dreams of identity politics. But the daytime dreams
of possibility, of social transformation, have their dark side—as the
briefest glance at international politics shows; dreamt at night, the
dreams of identity politics are nightmares of despair. (This points to
the simultaneous existence of both the vivifying claims of identity and
the murderous results of those claims across the geopolitical map.)*

4. CULTURAL TRANSLATION AND THE LOCATIONS OF EXPERIENCE

*I want to return now briefly to the question of the relations within
feminism between deconstruction and identity or experience politics,
more specifically to the issue of positive or undecided identities, singular or multiple. What follows below is an excerpt from an interview
conducted with Barbara Johnson published in 1987. Johnson, who is
known first as a post-structuralist (de Manian) critic, and only more
recently as a feminist one, is asked how her mode of deconstruction is
affected by her being a woman.*

> Johnson: I think women are socialized to see more than one
> point of view at a time, and certainly to see more than
> their own point of view. It seems to me that women
> are all trained, to some extent, to be deconstructors.
> There's always a double message, and there's always

a double response. The difficulty, for women, is un-learning self-repression and ambiguation and concili-ation, and reaching affirmation. For me, there are two things going on in the place I am at, right now, in criticism. One is definitely that I've gone as far as I want to go with opening up ambiguities. I need to attach that kind of consideration to questions whose answer cannot simply be, "It's undecidable." At the same time, I find that a lot of feminist criticism is very shy of ambiguity, not interested in undecidability, even as a provisional exploratory situation. So my tendency would be to inject more suspension of an-swer into feminist criticism, rather than less. But I realize that that goes along with female socialization, rather than against it.

Imre Salusinszky: What do you have in mind as the sorts of question which cannot *be* undecidable?

Johnson: Places where it begs the question to say "It's undecid-able." If you were reading a text, like, say, Zora Neale Hurston's "How It Feels to Be Colored Me" [which Johnson has done], at the end you can say that the text does not give you an answer to that title; it doesn't tell you; it really shows that the whole thing is undecidable and cannot be formulated in that way. But you know that you've only gone so far, by saying that. You have not, at all, accounted for the fact of racism, the fact of disadvantageous conditions of life. So that's not a satisfying place to stop with such an investigation. What you would have to figure out is how to ask questions that would *take* the impossibil-ity of answering a question like that, alongside the social system that acts as if there is an answer, and then analyze the relations between those two (169–70).

In the philosopher's dream of the innumerable, I argued, the subjects of the dance are staged in an oneiric choreography in which they perform outside any recognizable frame of reference; they pirouette beyond all local contingencies of history and place. Even though Derrida's reflection on feminism takes as its pretext McDonald's invocation of "maverick feminist" (as she is referred to by both of them) Emma Goldman's remark, "If I can't dance I don't want to be part of your revolution": *the question of social revolution in his text is finally displaced, overshadowed by the desire to escape the two of sexual difference* ("what remains undecidable concerns not only but also the line of cleavage between the two sexes" *[75]*).

Against the dream of "incalculable choreographies," let me propose a last dream passage: the dream of a feminist critic for whom the dream never escapes the social. This is the end of Rich's well-known 1971 essay, "When We Dead Awaken":

> In closing I want to tell you about a dream I had last summer. I dreamed I was asked to read my poetry at a mass women's meeting, but when I began to read, what came out were the lyrics of a blues song. I share this dream with you because it seemed to me to say something about the problems and the future of the woman writer, and probably of women in general. The awakening of consciousness is not like the crossing of a frontier—one step and you are in another country (48).

In a footnote to this passage added in 1978, Rich asks herself: "When I dreamed that dream, was I wholly ignorant of the tradition of Bessie Smith and other women's blues lyrics which transcended victimization to sing of resistance and independence?" *Like the philosopher who wonders where the* "'dream' of the innumerable would come from, if it is indeed a dream" *(76), and the poet who had already discovered that* "poems are like dreams: in them you put what you don't know you know" *(40), the dream of feminist critics, I think, already includes some linguistic knowledge of the culture of another country, even if we haven't traveled there. If, however, to circle back to our beginnings, for women, the dream is the truth, and women act and do things accordingly, then what remains is to do the work of the dream. This is an effect of what the Italian feminists call "self-consciousness," and that in the United States used to be called "consciousness raising." This involves, as Teresa de Lauretis argues, an attentiveness to experience,* "a political-personal strategy of survival and resistance that is also, at the same time, a critical practice and a mode of knowledge" (*Feminist Studies/Critical Studies*, 9).

But on this, I give Hurston the last word: as her experienced heroine Janie explains to Pheoby, who remains in speechless awe of her friend's narrative at the end of the novel, "It's uh known fact, Pheoby, you got tuh *go* there tuh *know* there."

II: Personal Histories, Autobiographical Locations

I had no place for Jews in the map of my thoughts.
—Minnie Bruce Pratt, "Identity: Skin Blood Heart"

"Boy, the food at this place is really terrible."
"Yeah, I know. And such small portions."
—Woody Allen, *Annie Hall*

In *"Feminist Politics: What's Home Got to Do with It?"* Biddy Martin and Chandra Mohanty elaborate a reading of Minnie Bruce Pratt's autobiographical narrative "Identity: Skin Blood Heart" that they see as an important instance of new ways of moving "individual self-reflection and critical practice" into the "building of political collectivity" (210). (Pratt's essay is one of three that make up the volume Yours in Struggle: Three Perspectives on Anti-Semitism and Racism.) The "'unity' of the individual subject, as well as the unity of feminism," Martin and Mohanty write, "is situated and specified as the product of interpretation of personal histories; personal histories that are themselves situated in relation to the development within feminism of particular questions and critiques" (192). The essay interests Martin and Mohanty primarily as a site on which the questions of "experience, identity, and political perspective" (192), which are the questions of feminist theory, are staged in productive ways. In particular, they focus on the interventionist advantages of Pratt's account.

The two critics read the current moment in feminist theory, indeed in Theory "itself," as a scene of competing emphases and investments. Notably, they analyze the tensions between what some see as a depoliticized poststructuralist aesthetics and a humanist (liberal) propensity for (re)universalization. They point specifically to the "charges of totalization that come from the ranks of antihumanist intellectuals." *But they also argue that* "without denying the importance of their vigilante attacks on humanist beliefs in 'man' and Absolute Knowledge wherever they appear, it is equally important to point out the political implications of an insistence on 'indeterminacy' which implicitly, when not explicitly, denies the critic's own situatedness in the social, and in effect refuses to acknowledge the critic's own institutional home" *(193–94). In the case of a* "personal historical narrative," *it is not possible, Martin and Mohanty assert,* "to speak from, or on behalf of, an abstract indeterminacy." *By its very groundedness, its* "collapsing of author and text, its unreflected authorial intentionality, and its claims to personal and political authenticity," *a text like Pratt's would seem to embody the antithesis of deconstructive values:* "the assumption that difference can emerge only through self-referential language" *(194). Indeed, against the fiction of split subjects constructed by the signifiers of their own alterity,* "Identity" *appears as a text firmly situated in the social and whose subject emerges from its locational politics. But in their reading of a narrative that, they want to show, by its emphases on identity in fact interrogates the very identity politics that deconstructive critics have placed under suspicion, Martin and Mohanty make another turn. As Martin put the matter in an oral presentation on Joan Nestle's* Restricted Country, *what interests her in these contemporary personal narratives of identity experience is this paradox: that in their insistence on singularity, these texts produce a new form of exchange between the theoretical and the personal. Put most sharply, Martin's point is that these narratives* "undo identity on the grounds of identity itself."[8]

Pratt's essay, which records the trajectory of a southern white lesbian through racism and anti-semitism, is structured through memory, the memory of places, of feelings attached to childhood places, and especially to her father (24–25). And like many of the writers in "Whose

Dream?" Pratt's reflection often passes through the language of dreams and nightmares. In the political work she does in the early days of women's liberation, she finds herself thinking that she had refound the ethos of that emotional location, a scene "without . . . violence, without . . . domination." *But her dreams tell another story:*

> I began to dream my husband was trying to kill me, that I was running away with my children on Greyhound buses through Mississippi. I began to dream that I was crossing a river with my children; women on the other side, but no welcome for me with my boys (25).

The bad dream comes true, at least in part. According to the ruling in her divorce, Pratt was not to have "a home with my children again" *(27). She* "could be either a lesbian or a mother of my children, either in the wilderness or on holy ground, but not both" *(26). Although as the narrative progresses, Pratt keeps moving forward toward that place of memory to be refound (52) with the* "exhilaration" *produced by the movement, by not succumbing to the inertia of old scenes, in the struggles of the experience to work through identity she is haunted by her father's claims on her. Martin and Mohanty comment:* "There is no shedding the literal fear and figurative law of the father, and no reaching a final realm of freedom. There is no new place, no new home" *(201). And yet the narrative ends with a dream of possibility, reminiscent in its cadences of the utopian passages we have just seen.*

> For years I have had a recurring dream: sleeping, I am reconciled to a woman from whom I have been parted: my mother, the Black woman who raised me, my first woman lover, a Jewish woman friend; in the dream we embrace, with the sweetness that can come in a dream when all is made right. I catch a glimpse of this possibility in my dream; it comes, in waking life, with my friends sometimes, with my lover: not an easy reconciliation, but one that may come when I continue the struggle with myself and the world I was born in (57).

Martin and Mohanty preface their essay with a gesture of autobiographical location:

> We began working on this project after visiting our respective "homes" in Lynchburg, Virginia and Bombay, India in the fall of 1984—visits fraught with conflict, loss, memories, and desires we both considered to

Dreaming, Dancing

be of central importance in thinking about our relationship to feminist politics. In spite of significant differences in our personal histories and academic backgrounds, and the displacements we both experience, the political and intellectual positions we share made it possible for us to work on, indeed to write, this essay together (191).

This is all we learn from and about the authors directly, though we are invited to find them in the text: "Just as Pratt refuses the methodological imperative to distinguish between herself as actual biographical referent and her narrator, we have at points allowed ourselves to let our reading of the text speak for us" (194). What is the effect of this postmodern resistance to establishing clearly the site of critical authority? Does the reader need to know where the critic-as-author stands in relation to her reading? Her pressure points?

This position of identification/nonidentification, the suspension of the autobiographical referent was also the strategy that I adopted in "Whose Dream?": letting my reading of the text through the juxtaposition of quotations "at points" speak for me. But as things turned out— on the occasions in which I performed this reading—the relation of critic to text proved to be too important a matter of authority to support that degree of textual ambiguity. To talk about the problems of Beckett *interpretation and reception produced by the "politics of quotation," I want to return now precisely— autobiographically—to the occasion of the conference, "Feminism and the Dream of a Plural Culture," with which I began.*

Part of the reason why I had decided to present an experimental paper at this event was that I had expected—in a singularly dramatic instance of miscommunication—to be speaking to a small gathering of faculty (and some of their students) who had been working on problems of critical theory together. I had assumed a certain commonality of reference and therefore a shared fund of citational practice. I arrived to find not a small working group but an auditorium filled with people— students, members of the community, a vast and heterogeneous scene. As if in response to the size and excitement of the audience, Bell Hooks, as the keynote speaker, left the podium, microphone in hand, and

93

virtually joined the audience in an improvised and inspirited conversa-
tion in which she expressed both her own wish as a feminist to write
not in an academic voice, but in a language her mother could read,
and her (rhetorical?) wish for us—the speakers—to abandon the texts
we had prepared, renounce academic protocol, and just talk to each
other.

To be sure, as the morning unfolded none of the speakers threw her
paper away—I clung to mine for dear life—but rarely have I wished
so intensely to jump ship and go home. As I stood there reading my
montage of quotations to this large and largely unresponsive (except
for the mass exodus, that is) audience, I felt that I had not only failed
to produce a vocabulary for talking about differences (the charge of
the conference agenda), but that I had somehow unwittingly violated
the spirit of the occasion. Despite my attempt through the play of
quotation to push at the edges of academic genre by relinquishing the
authority of a critical "I" that would guide and control the reading, I
had succeeded mainly, it seemed, in finding exactly the wrong tone
(perhaps the marker of the very control I played at relinquishing).
Because there was no time for discussion, moreover, I don't know
whether there might have finally been a way on that platform to
translate my project into another lexicon, to renegotiate positionings.
Bell Hooks, who was also to have been the respondent to the panel, told
me privately in passing that she would have wanted in her comments to
point to the commonalities among our papers. But this was not to be,
and for my part I left with a sense of the unbridgeability of certain
differences—at least in that setting, that setup, in which I became by
the structure of the event and by my own discursive position (to use
the language of my paper) and style the other of oppression: the straight
white woman.[9] The effect of quotation—texts concatenated without
contexts—designed to unsettle alignments through the play of language
reinforced them instead.[10]

Can a reading of the text speak for its reader? Such, at least, was my
gamble in assembling quotations (the montage was both a form of
reading— reading across a certain cultural horizon—and a writing).
Because in practice (on the occasion of my performance in Queens)

that did not seem sufficient; or, put another way, since the disembodiment of that position seemed to work against my own desire for a dialogics within feminism, I decided that in my revisions of the work I would place myself— autobiographically—in relation to the material of identity already elaborated through the quotations.[11] *More specifically, wanting to fracture the simplified profile of straight white woman, and in the spirit of a more locational feminist politics, I placed myself in the text "as a Jew." This self-identification took two forms in the essay: the first, an anecdotal account of identity politics within the institution; the second, the inclusion of quotations about dreams and nightmares in Israel and Palestine.*

I began by recalling my experience teaching the Pratt essay "Identity" in a seminar on feminist theory at the Graduate Center. "I had no place for Jews in the map of my thoughts," Pratt writes, "except that they had lived before Christ in an almost mythical Israel, and afterwards in Germany until they were killed, and that those in this country were foreign, even if they were here: they were always foreign, their place was always somewhere else"(31). In the process of teaching this piece, I suddenly realized that I was the only Jew in the room and that reading "my Jewish lover" embodied and fixed in the turns of Pratt's rhetoric made me intensely uncomfortable. I didn't like reading the (negative) signifiers—Jews/foreign/somewhere else—and then feeling interpellated as "the Jewish woman" in the record of this white woman's awakening (working her anti-semitism through "on" me). I didn't say much, if anything, about it at the time—being the teacher—and I think now that this was an error of pedagogy. Not only because "counting Jews" (which I often do despite myself) might have in useful ways complicated the terms of our discussion in itself, but because I think my feeling othered, interpellated, really, by this solemn celebration of the other was also a response to a failure in the writing: the shifting line between the poignancy of self-representation and the didactics of representativity that needed analysis.

My reaction to the rhetoric of identity and difference in the Pratt essay (irritation and silence) brought me back to a dramatic moment at the conference on feminist theory in Milwaukee in 1985 that Teresa de Lauretis organized in which Evelyn Torton Beck exhorted Jewish women to identify themselves (take back their names and their noses) and wondered aloud from the platform, aggressively, polemically, why Jewish (better yet, Yiddish), female-authored texts were not taught in Women's Studies courses alongside Chicana, Native American, etc. works as "ethnic" or "minority" literature (which is a fair enough question). Sondra O'Neale, a black critic on the panel, had replied, equally polemically and upping the ante, that Jews had no right to speak of oppression or marginality since, unlike blacks, they could "choose to pass." At which point Blanche Gelfand rose from the audience to observe that six million of them seemed to have failed to exercise that option. Gayatri Spivak, another of the panelists, urged the audience to remember their Palestinian sisters, who were not with us, and whose men were dying. I sat there, in silent shock at the turn this politically correct occasion was taking, not saying anything, and waiting for it to be over. What was there, really, to say once the structure of competing oppressions had been put in place in those terms?[12]

But what would it have meant then, mean now for me, to speak "as a Jew," as a Jewish woman?: I who have never visited that "almost mythical place Israel," and whose most vivid daily (and not, therefore, entirely trivial) cultural sense of being Jewish is inseparable from being a New Yorker (if not theorized, at least revisited by Woody Allen).[13] In the version of the piece I circulated at the School of Criticism and Theory, I went on to sketch the outlines of an assimilated Jewish childhood in New York, and then segued (hurtled myself, is more like it, over an abyss of questions about being Jewish and the state of Israel, Israel before and after 1967, the question of a Palestinian state, etc.) into long passages excerpted from David Grossman's Yellow Wind, *a writer I admire. This material—an Israeli psychiatrist's account of the dreams of Arab and Israeli children that ended my essay without further comment from me—generated a reaction in the audience that brought me up abruptly against both my personal anxieties about speaking "as a Jew" and the dangerous ambiguity, underlined by*

Dreaming, Dancing

Edward Said, produced by the politics of quotation itself. (The agonies of Middle-East politics aside, it's true that I should have thought twice about giving a psychiatrist the last word, especially in a paper about dreams!)

Did being Jewish really mean I always *wanted to speak "as a Jew" and be spoken as one? The short answer is no, I have not found a way to assume that rhetoric of identity (although I am both, I cannot lay claim to "Jewish feminist"); it is not a ground of action for me in the world, nor the guarantee of my politics—or writing.[14] The fact, however, of being both Jewish and a feminist is a crucial, even constitutive piece of my self-consciousness as a writer; and in that sense of course it is also at work—on occasion—in the style and figures of my autobiographical project.*

In order to represent the crisis in contemporary feminist cultural theory, I had wanted to produce a meta-critical fiction whose author would spin off into the interstices between the acts. But allowing my reading of the quotations to speak for me without signing them (evaluating them and historicizing them, as the phrase goes, against each other) turned out to mean letting readers read for me—which meant their placing, identifying, and worst of all, perhaps, misreading me: in my own text, in my place. Placing myself in the text after the fact as a nameable identity proved an even greater failure.

To some extent the difficulty of these two occasions was an effect of context; it was also, and more importantly, a symptom of the project of identity writing itself: impossible to elude: the co-implication, which always seems to find its borders in violence, of the "speaking as a"s and "speaking for"s . . . It is for this reason that I have not tried, even in this space of written revision, to master the crisis by a conclusion that would put things back together again. This could only be done by a discourse of containment that depends finally on making an abstraction of that violence.

The narrative of these occasions is necessarily locational: it is what happens to theory in the flesh of practice, in the social spaces of institutional life.

97

Getting Personal

That narrative is also necessarily autobiographical.
The questions before us in critical theory might go something like
this: can we imagine a self-representational practice—for feminism—
that is not recontained by the pre-constituted tropes of representativity?
How do the cultural and political constraints that provide the context
for our discussions police and shortcircuit their effects?

NOTES

I want to thank Anthony O'Brien and Nancy Comley for enlisting my participation in the conference at Queens College.

I would also like to thank Danielle Haase-Dubosc for getting me to Paris and Rosi Braidotti to Utrecht where I presented Part One of this essay. I am equally grateful to Patricia Cholakian and Nancy Rabinowitz for the opportunity to discuss this material at a conference called "Feminism for the Year 2000," held at Hamilton College, and to colleagues at Endicott College, New Jersey.

1. This is expressed in the title of Catharine R. Stimpson's collection of essays, *Where the Meanings Are: Feminism and Cultural Spaces*, and in that of the new journal *differences*, edited by Naomi Schor and Elizabeth Weed, which describes itself as "a journal of feminist cultural studies"; feminist and cultural perspectives come together as well in the volume of essays collected by Susan Sheridan in *Grafts*, which bears the subtitle *Feminist Cultural Criticism*.

2. Diana Fuss's *Essentially Speaking* provides a thorough and illuminating account of this phenomenon.

3. Denise Riley begins her essay *"Am I That Name?": Feminism and the Category of "Women" in History* with a recasting of that polarization. "It's my hope to persuade readers," she argues, "that a new Sojourner Truth might well—except for the catastrophic loss of grace in the wording—issue another plea: 'Ain't I a fluctuating identity?' For both a concentration on and a refusal of the identity of 'women' are essential to feminism" (1).

4. This is very much the project, I think, of Trinh T. Minh-ha's *Woman, Native, Other,* whose use of quotation is further complicated by the use of graphics and photos.

5. Ann Cooper Albright, a dancer and critic, has written interestingly on the metaphorics of the dance in feminist theory in "Incalculable Choreographies" (this is a chapter of a dissertation for the Performance Studies Department at NYU, "Mining the Dancefield: Feminist Theory and Contemporary Dance"). She tells me that I'm all wrong about Pina Bausch; that she's just Balanchine revamped for an audience enamored of the "avant-garde."

6. In *Coming of Age in Mississippi*, Anne Moody writes: "By the time we got to the

Lincoln Memorial, there were already thousands of people there. I sat on the grass and listened to the speakers, to discover we had 'dreamers' instead of leaders leading us. Just about every one of them stood up there dreaming. Martin Luther King went on and on talking about his dream. I sat there thinking that in Canton we never had time to sleep, much less dream" (307).

7. In the context of his reply to Barbara Christian's "The Race for Theory," Michael Awkward unexpectedly rereads/retrieves Smith's essay *for* poststructuralism by shifting the emphasis in her argument from representations of a lesbian text to the constructions of a lesbian reader (240–42).

8. In "Lesbian Identity and Autobiographical Difference(s)" (1989), Martin looks at this and other texts in which the question of identity is the primary mode of self-representation, and (following Teresa de Lauretis's notion of "micropolitical practices") argues that the texts "work against self-evidently homogeneous conceptions of identity" (82). For Martin, autobiographical writings like Pratt's and the pieces collected in *This Bridge* "serve as a concrete example of how the politics of identity has been challenged on its very grounds" (82). This would be an "authority of experience" in which both experience and authority have been radically worked over: turned inside out, and emptied of an earlier empirically naive conception of "women" (81); in their complication these self-productions announce a "theory in the flesh" (96). Despite de Lauretis's and Martin's seductive account of the complexities that shape these writings, I feel that the politics of experience at work in oppositional self-naming—women of color/white women, lesbian/straight women necessarily produces structuring effects of identification (or disidentification) in the reader: certainly in me. Perhaps this is a function of the autobiographical act.

9. The line was drawn neatly, I thought, when at one moment in her paper, Barbara Omolade quoted Hortense Spillers—whom I had also cited in my montage—as "Sister Spillers."

10. In order to work against the exclusionary effects of quotations that seem disoriginated and disembodied, in subsequent presentations of this material I distributed a handout with the text of the quotations. This at least mitigated the difficulty of listening to and trying to follow long quotations by people one might not have heard of.

11. Before I revised that version of "Whose Dream?" I had the opportunity to rehearse it in the context of the "Feminism in the Year 2000" conference. The agenda for the occasion in fact solicited an autobiographical frame and perspective on these problems:

Has feminism become old-fashioned? Do we need to abandon the term in order to move forward? What will be the theoretical language of the future? Does the so-called feminist, poststructuralist discourse have a place in our work? What is to be done about some feminists' fear of, anxiety about, distrust for theory? Does the statement that there are only Feminism-s help? Can we make the divisions within feminism positive and a strength, or is the fragmentation, evidenced by the constitution of the acrimony of the sexuality debates, a permanent and devastating condition?

Getting Personal

Of course, you cannot answer all these questions, but we wanted to let you know the areas of concern to us. Perhaps it would be most effective if you each talked briefly (and autobiographically) about your own "journey," and then focused on the single most troubling issue for you. What is the critical issue for which we must find theoretical form in the next decade?

—Patricia Francis Cholakian/ Nancy Sorkin Rabinowitz

12. In "Homelands of the Mind: Jewish Feminism and Identity Politics," Jenny Bourne provides an astringent analysis of these clotted issues; see especially 11-16.

13. I realize this sounds flippant. It's not all there is to it, but I want at least to introduce another register of cultural identity.

Jenny Bourne comments in her dissection of these difficulties: "There is, in the end, no stable diaspora-based identity for us as Jewish feminists; all roads seem one way or another to lead back to the question of Israel" (18). Having in fact visited Israel since writing this paper, I feel no closer to an understanding of the question.

14. I contrast this to the position Alicia Ostriker (reviewing the book) describes as Judith Plaskow's in *Standing at Sinai*: "I am not a Jew in the synagogue and a feminist in the world," Plaskow writes. "I am a Jewish feminist and a feminist Jew in every moment of my life" (12).

7

Philoctetes' Sister: Feminist Literary Criticism and the New Misogyny

The design for the plenary sessions for the "Conference on Narrative Literature" for which I wrote this essay included a crisscrossing of critical response among the speakers. The effects of that structure, I think, had a lot to do with the liveliness and intensity of the occasion. Unlike the "Conference on Narrative," which was not a thematically feminist event, "Double Trouble," the other occasion I want to acknowledge here, was organized to mark the formal inauguration (complete with academic robes) of two chaired professorships in Women's Studies at the University of Utrecht. In both cases, however, beyond the remarkable intellectual performances of the other speakers, what made these scenes especially important for me— personally—was the chance to receive pointed and imaginative (even, at times, perverse) readings of my work, which I have briefly taken up in the body of the essay. (D. A. Miller responded to my paper at Madison; my respondent in Utrecht was Maaike Meijer.)

I. DID PHILOCTETES HAVE A SISTER?

In "School-Time," the second book of *The Mill on the Floss*, Maggie Tulliver visits her brother Tom, who has been sent away to school for what their father calls "a good eddication: an eddication as'll be a bread to him" (56). What this means to Mr. Tulliver emerges in a conversation he has with Mr. Riley, a gentleman (and auctioneer) who has impressed Tulliver with his learning, and who is advising him in the proper choice of school. To Riley's question about Tom's intelligence, Tulliver replies:

"Well, he isn't not to say stupid—he's got a notion o' things out o' door, an' a sort o' commonsense, as he'd lay hold o' things by the right handle. But he's slow with his tongue, you see, and he reads but poorly, and can't abide the books, and spells all wrong, they tell me, an' as shy as can be wi' strangers, an' you never hear him say 'cute things like the little wench. Now, what I want is, to send him to a school where they'll make him a bit nimble with his tongue and his pen, and make a smart chap of him. I want my son to be even wi' these fellows as have got the start o' me with having better schooling" (69).

On the first day of Maggie's visit, Tom proves as clumsy laying hold of things by the right handle as with his tongue (moving his lips as he reads his Latin lessons). Trying to impress his sister with his prowess by impersonating the Duke of Wellington, he drops the sword he has been waving about—heroically, he hopes—on his foot and faints dead away from the pain. Tom's accident, which he briefly fears will leave him lame, brings him unexpectedly (and as briefly) closer to his more intellectually gifted schoolmate, Philip Wakem. Philip, who reads Greek with pleasure—this impresses Maggie and baffles Tom—has in the past entertained Tom with what Tom calls "fighting stories," and on this occasion, he tells Tom and Maggie the story of Philoctetes, "a man who had a very bad wound in his foot, and cried out so dreadfully with the pain, that his friends could bear with him no longer, but put him ashore on a desert island, with nothing but some wonderful poisoned arrows to kill animals with for food" (258–59). Maggie and Tom have different reactions to Philip's narrative about the lame man: Tom claims that *he* didn't roar out with pain; Maggie feels that it is permissible to cry out when injured, but her response to the story is finally less a reaction to the accident itself than to its consequences, the lame man's abandonment on the island: "She wanted to know," Eliot's narrator writes, "if Philoctetes had a sister, and why *she* didn't go with him on the desert island and take care of him" (259). (I will return to Maggie's question.)

In "The Wound and the Bow," Edmund Wilson reflects upon the legend of Philoctetes as dramatized by Sophocles. Wilson begins his reflection by observing that the play is "far from being his most popular," and the "myth itself . . . not . . . one of those which have excited the modern imagination" (223). The *Philoctetes,* Wilson argues early in the essay, "assigns itself . . . to a category even more special and less generally appealing [than that of *Le Misanthrope* to which he compares its psychological conflict] through the fact . . . that the conflict is not even allowed to take place between a man and a woman." Commenting on the limited "imprint of the play on literature since the Renaissance," perhaps because of its exclusive focus on the relations between men, Wilson cites the example of a "French dramatist of the seventeenth century, Chateaubrun, [who] found the subject so inconceivable that, in trying to concoct an adaptation which would be acceptable to the taste of his time . . . provided Philoctetes with a daughter named Sophie with whom Neoptolemus was to fall in love and thus bring the drama back to the reliable and eternal formula of Romeo and Juliet and the organizer who loves the factory-owner's daughter" (224).

My concern here is not to determine whether Philoctetes really had a sister, a daughter, or even a mother—though we can, I suppose, feel rather more certain about the last. Nor by my emphasis on Maggie's creation of a woman in the text am I advocating an "ethics of care" (in Carol Gilligan's terms) or a "poetics of need" (in Lawrence Lipking's). I want to suggest instead that like the feminist critic at the end of the twentieth century, reading against the doxa of indifference and its institutional exclusions, Maggie imagines a sister for Philoctetes and inserts herself in a story otherwise notable, as Wilson points out, for being "devoid of feminine interest" in order to place herself as a subject of cultural narrative. Maggie had already bumped up against the codes of gender in her first visit to Mr. Stelling's school. She had pondered the example in her brother's Latin Grammar of the "astronomer who hated women," wondering whether "all astronomers hated women, or whether it was only this particular astronomer." She concluded without waiting for the teacher's answer: "I suppose it's all astronomers: because you know, they live up in high towers, and if the women came there, they might talk and hinder them from looking at the stars" (220). On the heels of this mournful interpretation, she had heard Mr. Stelling pronounce, to her brother's immense satisfaction, that girls had "a great deal of superficial cleverness," but that "they couldn't go far into anything. They're quick and shallow" (220–21). Maggie, whose father had earlier lamented to Mr. Riley the "topsy-turvy world" which produces "stupid lads and 'cute wenches" (68–69), and who will not be sent away to Mr. Stelling's to learn Latin or Greek, returns home after her visit, reduced to silence by the prospect of "this dreadful destiny" (221).

Feminist critics over almost two decades have debated the matter of the astronomers and their hatred of women in particular and in general. Mary Jacobus, in a discussion of the politics of women's writing, has offered an especially rewarding reading of misogyny in these passages and the staging in Eliot's novel of the "question of women's access to knowledge and culture and to the power that goes with them" (68). But let us leave the *Mill* and turn now instead to the misogyny of the new astronomers—the Stellings of contemporary literary life in academia; I want to look specifically at the *language* of their reactions to the feminist critics who have pursued in different ways the implications in literature and in culture of the "dreadful destiny" reserved for girls like Maggie Tulliver: the thwarted life and early death—to pick a fable dear to literary feminism—of Shakespeare's sister famously imagined by Virginia Woolf.

2. A REPORT FROM THE ACADEMY, OR THE NEW ASTRONOMY

In the fall of 1988, *The American Scholar* (the organ of Phi Beta Kappa) published an essay called "Feminist Literary Criticism" (and subtitled "A Report from the Academy"). Its author, Peter Shaw, identified as "the author of the forthcoming *The War Against the Intellect: Episodes in the Decline of Discourse,*" begins his report with an epigraph from Virginia Woolf: "The greatest writers lay no stress upon sex one way or the other. The critic is not reminded as he reads them that he belongs to the masculine or feminine gender."[1] The choice of epigraph is important, for it appropriates—at the threshold of a hostile review of feminist criticism—the signature of feminist criticism's "foremother," who appears here to authorize the dismissal of one of literary feminism's central questions: the relation of gender to the reading and writing of literature and criticism. Through Woolf the critic both separates himself from the challenge of feminist criticism— having to remember as he reads the effects of a social identity consti- tuted in gender—and universalizes his position through his adherence to the canons: "the greatest writers."

This is not an especially original essay—it is very reminiscent in its basic moves of the Denis Donoghue 1986 attack on feminist criticism: a generic trashing, we might say—but its interest for us here resides precisely in its patronizing familiarity.[2] "Feminist Literary Criticism" marks the reincrustation of an updated misogyny—the refusal to ac- knowledge the epistemological and cultural constructions of sexual difference—within a certain (we're all human) mainstream. I think it's worth attending to this renewal of discursive misogyny—directed at feminists on behalf of women!—as part of a general movement of reactionary gestures within a variety of institutional contexts.[3]

The report begins with what its author takes to be the "most trouble- some" question within feminist criticism today: "whether or not wom- en's writing differs in some essential way from men's" (67). Like Donoghue's, this irascible humanist's difficulty with feminist criticism is intimately bound up with what he calls, placing it between quotation marks, "critical theory." "This term," he writes, "which once simply designated theorizing about literature, has of course come to refer to the range of French-derived, post-structuralist theories of which the best known is deconstruction. Feminist critics," he goes on to claim, "among others, appear to have borrowed the recherché vocabulary of post-structuralism chiefly as a handy form of certification in today's theory-ridden academy . . ." (71). In this chronology, we are now witnessing a Stage Three of "gender theory" which owes its particular tone to its adoption of "critical theory." He then addresses the "trou- blesome question" that constitutes the internal failure of this phase of feminist criticism. "The trouble came with the attempt to make a case for an essential gender difference in the act of writing. For exactly where, they were forced to ask, can gender be identified as crucial in writing? Does it manifest itself in plot? In style? In setting?" (71) (It is an intriguing fact that whenever a critic of feminism wants to criticize feminist theories or practices as being essentialist, s/he—I of course include female critics as well—in turn essentializes the representation by using the terms "essential," "essentially.")

As opposed to the feminist quest for "an essential gender difference in the act of writing" that reads self-consciously *for* the operations of gender in cultural narratives, the humanist defends the old values of transparency: the apprehension of an art outside the pressures of ideology. The critic in that story, a cultivated reader at home in a library of great books, needs to understand of a work only what is self-evidently there; the critic's task is to supply "a satisfactory account of the aesthetic object." The critical elaboration of this account, the argument goes, constitutes a poetics of "moral action," a practice that eschews politics: it is a reading without an agenda, enlisted in the service of art itself. Although such a poiesis is difficult, the failure to share the difficulty of a *beyond politics* as a goal is what shocks in the work of feminist critics. Granted, an "unintended bias" has always accompanied literary criticism; but being "inadvertently influenced by politics" is one thing; to *choose* "subordination to its aims and principles" is a failure of "social morality"—like "cheating at cards."[4] "Feminist critics . . . have repudiated the morality of the aesthetic. . . . Until and unless feminist criticism commits itself to aesthetic value, one can predict, it will continue to turn in on itself, repudiating one stage after another of necessarily inadequate theory" (85). To the extent that feminist criticism is by definition an ethical project, and as such bound to a "morality of the aesthetic" that *includes* aesthetics' ethical contexts (the very sort that Woolf, precisely, understood as integral to a humane apprehension of art) it is difficult to imagine that we stand a chance with our humanist.

But exactly what politics, one might well wonder, have undermined feminist criticism? "Mainstream liberal feminist criticism," we read, "has allowed itself to be taken intellectually hostage by French structuralist biologism, . . . Marxism, white and black lesbianism, and other radical forms of expression" (86). The remaining mainstream, liberal, heterosexual (presumably), bourgeois (white and black, one assumes) feminists—who have escaped hijacking by these dangerous others, and who are still reading the essay—should renounce their alliances with "political radicals" and rededicate themselves to the arduous apprenticeship of aesthetic value: art for the sake of art.[5] But would that go far enough?

The heart of the matter comes in the final paragraph of the essay where the promise of the epigraph is fulfilled:

> The one broad avenue to participation in the life of the culture always thought to have been open to women—literature's noble republic of the spirit—is in one way or another effectively denied women by feminist criticism. Yet it was through literature that Mary Ann Evans, writing as George Eliot, could confront her world unfettered by any limitations that might be thought to attach to her as a woman. Through literature Emily Dickinson and Willa Cather were free to write poems and stories in which the "I" who speaks is male rather than female, thereby claiming their privilege to speak for any kind of human being their imaginations were capable of grasping . . . . In a field where women's excellence is incontestable, feminist literary critics, starting out in the conviction that women writers had long suffered at the hands of male critics, have ended up fostering an image of women at least as insulting as any that they set out to protest (87).

In the celebration of a universal subjectivity in art, the old (we hoped, moribund) tenets of lit.crit.-bashing are resuscitated by an attack on feminist critics cast as a defense of women and culture.[6] Through literature, and more specifically through the use of the male pseudonym and male personae, women writers have been able to liberate themselves and attain a whole human experience.

What's "new" here—but of course misogyny is never really new—is the protection of women from their feminist sisters. By their insistence on the work of gender in culture (did Philoctetes have a sister, Mary Ann Evans wondered), on exposing the exclusions of women from the "broad avenue to participation in the life of the culture" (George Eliot freed Mary Ann Evans from being read "as a woman"), feminist critics have denied women the subjectivity of their fictional "I's" (writing "as a man").

They have also, it seems, denied male critics their fantasy-monopoly on human identity.

3. "READER, MY STORY ENDS WITH FREEDOM . . ."

In the law, rights are islands of empowerment.
 —Patricia Williams, "On Being the Object of Property"

In reading Joyce, one is reading Literature—Literature with a
capital L. The tide rises above the little figures islanded here
and there in a waste of waters, and gradually they disappear
till nothing is left but the blank expanse of Literature,
mirroring the blank face of the sky.
 —Frank O'Connor, *The Mirror in the Roadway*

In the broadside delivered against feminist criticism as a political
poetics, the argument assumes that the reading of literary texts can
and should be abstracted from the *reminder* of gender and that writing
about them should perform the same forgetting. In the presence of
great writing, the reader ideally forgets both the author's sex and his
own. I don't know whether the critic of feminist literary politics would
go on to make the same argument about black literary feminism and
the role played by race in cultural production: the common humanity
expressed and transcended through art in a severance from the social.
In the attack on feminist criticism described below, however, the argument connecting gender to race within cultural enactments is made
explicitly; and to put that politics of abstraction into bolder relief, I
want to begin with a critical reading that, like the text it illuminates,
forgets neither gender nor race.

In *Self-Discovery and Authority in Afro-American Narrative,* Valerie
Smith argues that the slave narrators of the nineteenth century, like
the "protagonist-narrators of certain twentieth-century novels by Afro-
American writers affirm and legitimize psychological autonomy by
telling the stories of their own lives." Her central point relies on the
"paradox," "that by fictionalizing one's life, one bestows a quality
of authenticity on it . . . [that] the processes of plot construction,
characterization, and designation of beginnings and endings—in short
the process of authorship— provide the narrators with a measure of

authority unknown to them in either real or fictional life." In this way, Smith maintains, "narrators not only grant themselves significance and figurative power over their superordinates, but in their manipulation of received literary conventions they also engage with and challenge the dominant ideology" (2).

In her discussion of Harriet Jacobs's autobiographical narrative, *Incidents in the Life of a Slave Girl,* Smith emphasizes the fundamental problem of form that confronts the author of a slave narrative. "When Jacobs asserts that her narrative is no fiction, that her adventures may seem incredible but are nevertheless true, . . . that only experience can reveal the abomination of slavery, she underscores the inability of her form adequately to capture her experience" (40). Jacobs, Smith remarks:

> invokes a plot initiated by Richardson's *Pamela,* and recapitulated in nineteenth-century American sentimental novels, in which a persistent male of elevated social rank seeks to seduce a woman of a lower class. Through her resistance and piety, she educates her would-be seducer into an awareness of his own depravity and his capacity for true, honorable love. In the manner of Pamela's Mr. B, the reformed villain rewards the heroine's virtue by marrying her (41).

The familiar rhetoric of this plot both enables and disables an effective representation of slavery in narrative. On the one hand, the effusive apostrophes to the reader, euphemistic language, and silence about sexual detail create a common reading ground with the white female readers Jacobs must address and persuade: and Jacobs is writing both to "engender additional abolitionist support" and move women readers in the North to action. But at the same time, Smith observes, the insistence on the structural similarity also trivializes the violence that inheres in slave experience. Pamela, after all, can escape to her parents' home, and have her "virtue rewarded" by marrying her master, and "elevating her and their progeny to his position" (37). By definition, or rather by the logic of slavery, the master does not marry his slave, and her posterity becomes another increment to his property.

But as Smith importantly shows, the tension between similarity and difference can produce a gain for narrative. When the reader arrives at the end of the autobiography and is addressed by the apostrophe "Reader, my story ends with freedom; not in the usual way, with marriage" Jacobs "calls attention to the space between the traditional happy ending of the novel of domestic sentiment and the ending of her story" (42). Unlike Jane Eyre, moreover, whose jubilant pre-closural address to the reader—"Reader, I married him"—has posed problems for feminist readers, and who like Pamela could marry her master and bear his child legitimately, Linda Brent—the pseudonym of Jacobs's first-person narrator—ends her story still questing for a "home": "The dream of my life is not yet realized. I do not sit with my children in a home of my own. I still long for a hearthstone of my own." Jacobs's text is constructed, we might say, in the gaps produced by that difference: the irreducible distance between slave reality and sentimental narrative, both of which finally remain authorized by patriarchy.

My account of Smith's argument has emphasized her analysis of the dramatic ways in which narrative commonalities allow us to take the measure of difference in readers: when, for instance, the white female reader who stops over "Reader, my story ends with freedom; not in the usual way, with marriage" perceives the difference race makes—that freedom for one who doesn't own oneself, comes from being sold, "*sold* at last"—she is reminded both of her gender and race. Should she as a critic seek to forget this?

In the summer of 1988, Valerie Smith and I participated in a certain number of events at the School of Criticism and Theory. Smith gave a lecture entitled "Gender and Afro-Americanist Literary Theory and Criticism" in which she addressed—among other things—the question of oppositional discourses and their relation to institutional contexts and constraints; I presented "Dreaming, Dancing, and the Changing Locations of Feminist Criticism."

In his reply to the arguments of this piece, the director of the School, Michael Riffaterre, a well-known semiotician, laid out before an audience of students and colleagues what he took to be the assumptions of my work as a feminist critic. The critique, while necessarily dependent on the existence of my person as a pre-text, identifies itself for the most part as being addressed to what is labeled (by him) in capital letters:

Feminist Criticism (hereafter, FC, by me). In what follows, I hope to show how the two takes on FC—the humanist's outcry and the semiotician's lament, which one might not have supposed to interpenetrate—in fact relay each other on a continuum of reaction: the discourse here of universal literary value, which in turn rejoins the earlier call for a "morality of the aesthetic."

Before reviewing the critique, I need to say a word about this mixed mode of autobiography and cultural analysis I'm calling narrative criticism. Although as I have just suggested, I figure in the story primarily as a convenient metonymy of FC (its Mary Beton, just as the reader may like to imagine the first critic as Woolf's Mr. A, whose phallic "I" casts a long shadow over the pages of his prose, and this one as the angry Professor Von X in *A Room of One's Own*), it's also the case that my account emerges from an institutional performance in which I coincided personally, as it were, with my representativity. My object in returning now to the critical material of that occasion, however— beyond the self-justification that comes with the territory of autobiography,[7] is to illuminate the network of theoretical assumptions about literature and literary criticism at the heart of the new astronomy.

The critic moves quickly to his main point, which is to challenge the "insularity of Feminist Criticism." He finds it "strange" that "the same people who would campaign against any form of male-enforced segregation or discrimination against women, or against any discrimination, and rightly so, should become segregationists in Feminist Criticism and discriminate against men as readers." Feminist critics, he complains, "are not content to define [our] difference, [we] are othering male critics . . . and excommunicating their interpretations." (Feminist critics are addressed through me as "you.") Explicitly or not, he maintains, we "posit that, being male, they cannot possibly understand or properly read a text that has been written by a woman for women." And, he concludes in the next sentence, "it is obvious that the premises of today's Black Criticism imply the same kind of exclusion."[8] What is one to make of the scenario that has male critics bodily prevented from reading women's writing and white critics from black writing? What feminist beadle has barred their access to the library? banned their books? banished their hermeneutics? Looking out across the cartography of our institutions, one can only wonder: *who left whom on the island?* And yet we need now to take a harder look at the language of othering that posits the exclusions and the relations between them: how are Feminist and Black Critics (or translated into the consecrated phrase of affirmative action, "women and minorities") alike and different? What is going on when feminists are accused of "segregation" in their attitudes toward male critics—a word intimately associated with the history of racism in this country? (More typically in anti-feminist rhetoric, feminists are accused of separatism, which in turn is of course a code word for lesbianism.)

The collapsing of distinctions in order to maximize their threat echoes the language of the most reactionary forces at work in the academy today (it is an emblem of eighties political culture). A recent example of the latter is Jon Wiener's account in the *Nation* (December 12, 1988) of a conference entitled "Reclaiming the Academy: Responses to the Radicalization of the University," calling for a "'renewed assertiveness' against feminism, ethnic studies and literary theory." The reporter quotes spokesperson Alan Kors, an intellectual historian from the University of Pennsylvania: "The immediate threat to academic freedom comes from antiharassment policies, racial awareness programs and the enshrinement of 'diversity' as a value for the university" (644).[9]

But let us return to the insularity of FC:

> Our duty as critics . . . is to explain and communicate. Furthermore, the only item that needs explaining to others and needs vicarious experiencing by them through the text is precisely the difference, be it gender, or class, or race. Why then, why start by saying that you cannot even succeed unless you own that difference by birthright? . . . Suppose we considered that metalinguistic features depending on gender, race, and class are unlikely ever to be erased, and that criticism by a native from the gender, race, or class under study might facilitate understanding. . . . Even if we were to concede that, the insularity of what I should call native criticism (rather than personal, or gender, or race criticism) would still ignore the very nature of the literary phenomenon, namely that it transcends time, place, and borders.

What would it mean to read *Incidents in the Life of a Slave Girl* as though its project transcended time, place, borders? Smith's poetics of slave narrative, as we have just seen, focuses on the tensions (and contradictions) between the representational demands of the slave narrative and narrative structures of self-fictionalization. But this attention to formal literary conventions also includes a critical awareness of "the political and economic context in which the texts have been produced." To ignore "the broad context in which [the texts] were written," Smith maintains, "invites misreading and denies their relation to the conditions and the sense of urgency that contributed to their very existence" (6). Does this mean that to read Jacobs's text *as* a slave narrative—a female-authored account of that historical experience— is to perform a "native criticism" that by definition "ignore[s] the very nature of the literary phenomenon"? To cite Smith one last time: "the critical work, no less than the artistic, bears the imprint of the conditions under which it was produced and articulates the writer's relation to culture" (7). This belief in cultural context, I would argue, is no more "insular"—you have to be black (a black woman) to "properly read" a black-authored text[10]—than the article of faith that circumscribes the text in order to seal its borders. In the case of *Incidents in the Life of a Slave Girl*, for example, if as a critic—black or white, male or female—you failed to explain the inscription of race and gender in the text's structures of address, your "account of the aesthetic object" (to invoke the terms of the argument rehearsed earlier) would by the same token overlook the "metalinguistic features" that give the text its generic specificity.

In other words, rather than adopting a discourse of the monument that rigidly opposes an inside ("the literary phenomenon") to an outside ("time, place, borders"), we need precisely a revisionary "morality of the aesthetic" that would produce a reading capable of interpreting, for instance, the marks of race and gender in the text as *intrinsic* to literariness itself. This would be another way of understanding the ethical project of feminist aesthetics.

The reading model according to which the critic radically divides literature from culture—as though we could ever be sure where to draw the line—seems condemned to the very insularity it seeks to locate outside its operations: to reproducing the politics of its location. Geographically this means not noticing, for instance, that continents are only very large islands . . . .

4. LEMNOS AND THE POLITICS OF INSULARITY

> There are those who say
> an array of horsemen,
> and others of marching men,
> and others of ships, is
> the most beautiful thing on the dark
> earth.
> But I say it is whatever one loves.
>
> —Sappho, 16 "On Helen"

Having arrived at this point in my narrative, I find myself wanting to tie up all the loose ends with a novelistic fabrication; a turn or twist of the plot, bringing us all, it all—Maggie, Philoctetes, the conservative backlash—to satisfying, if not sublime closure: marriage, or freedom, or Troy, or home. Reader, I . . . Reader, my story ends with . . . But how does it end? How do I want it to end?

We could return, for instance, to the matter left hanging in Maggie's question about Philoctetes' sister and her conviction that she would have cared for the wounded man left on the island, and have that figure for us a reflection about gendered plots, and specifically about the ways in which universal narratives—what Gayatri Spivak calls "regulative psychobiography" (227)—construct and are constructed by social and political agendas.

We could also observe that these othered male critics would prefer for feminists to be more like women (like Maggie) and look after their wounded heroes.

We might ponder the current academic debates about the status and effects of oppositional discourses; these are joined issues.

And we might even wonder whether there isn't a way in which, like Philoctetes, feminists have come to love their island and to look with great suspicion on the call (when it is not a demand) for them to return to the fatherland: for this is, I think, what the accusations of insularity, segregation, separatism, and feminist misogyny come down to.

Philoctetes, we recall, was abandoned by Odysseus and their comrades in arms almost ten years before the play begins. They left Philoctetes on the island of Lemnos because they couldn't take the smell of his stinking foot and the howls of pain his wound produced. Now, having learned from a prophecy that Troy can only be captured by Philoctetes' bow—a bow given to him by Heracles—Odysseus and Neoptolemus have come back to get the bow and the man. Philoctetes takes a dim view of rejoining the war at the behest of the man who had so cruelly abandoned him to fend for himself on this deserted island; even though the return to Troy includes the promise of a cure, Philoctetes would rather suffer his pain and then find solace on those terms. The crux of the play involves the persuasion of Philoctetes, a decision to leave the island for Troy that is accomplished only through the intervention of a god coming out of the machine: the appearance on stage of Heracles, who commands Philoctetes to pick up his bow and go back to the war.

The *Philoctetes* has attracted a great deal of critical attention and competing interpretations in recent years.[11] Following Carola Greengard's emphasis on the play's political dimensions, I will recast— for a postmodern feminist theater—the fable of the man on the island as a drama of political positioning.

Suppose, then, that we imagine the lonely Philoctetes on the island multiplied as a collective of feminist critics. They have been put on the island because they have been ruining life on the mainland; they keep complaining about their wound, and that *odor di femina* has been overpowering.[12] After the feminist critics have spent almost a decade of life in their Women's Studies community—we can just borrow some pages from Wittig's *Les Guérillères* to fill in the narrative here—the men (their former colleagues) decide they need them back. They've heard rumors, oracles that the feminists have unique knowledge that can help them with their students: enrollments are down, almost all the graduate students are female and demanding to read women's and minority writing (even the men want to be in feminism); their publishers are telling them to include women in their articles and their books. They send an emissary, not one of the old guard of course, but a younger representative (like Neoptolemus), one of the graduate students perhaps, or an assistant professor who does Theory.

Should the women return to save the institution? What faith can they have that promises will be met? If they can forgive past wrongs, can they expect no future ones? It has been painful in the wilderness, but also rewarding; they have forged new identities on the island that challenge the hierarchical conventions of the polis; these might not survive the return to the old war, the rules of a tarnished, virile heroism. In Sophocles' play, we should remember, it takes a god coming out of a machine to force Philoctetes' hand and bring him with his bow to Troy.

After almost two decades of FC, feminists—black and white—as well as other oppositional groups find themselves both marginalized (put on the island) for reasons of state and accused of insularity, of separatism, even "terrorism" (Ruthven, 10); othered and accused of othering; excluded and taxed with being exclusionary. As we enter the fin de siècle, of which much is already being made, the question of the islands and their "natives" will become more and not less acute.

You will by now have perceived at least one crucial difference between my drama and the legend of the man on the island. The difference is not sexual.[13] It is one of numbers: unlike Philoctetes, we are not alone on our islands. Odysseus, even supported by the gods and their prophecies, can less easily, in this post-colonial moment, make us an offer we can't refuse. We can look from our islands—not only to the main—but peripherally over at the other island people and propose what we would now call coalition politics, famously defined by Bernice Reagon as the antithesis of home: "You don't go into coalition because you just *like* it. The only reason you would consider trying to team up with somebody who could possibly kill you, is because that's the only way you can figure you can stay alive" (356–57). In that spirit we could chant some old radical cries of solidarity like "We are all Lemnians," hoping enough collective historical memory is left to make sense of it. But to end on that note would be to offer a solution that is already nostalgic.

Philoctetes, you recall, had no way to leave Lemnos on his own. As feminist critics we have acquired the freedom to move between the island and the mainland: we can leave and return, and we do.[14] Indeed the definition of feminist difference historically has been bound up with the movement between identities and locations; with the negotiations between scenes of power. Nonetheless, for us, as for Philoctetes, the stakes of negotiation remain high and require vigilance since we do not yet set the terms of the discussion. Nor is it clear that the gods are on our side.

Toward the end of "The Wound and the Bow," Wilson reads the *Philoctetes* allegorically: "The victim of a malodorous disease which renders him abhorrent to society and periodically degrades him and makes him helpless is also the master of a superhuman art which everybody has to respect and which the normal man finds he needs" (240). He then identifies the "more general and fundamental idea [of the play as]: the conception of superior strength as inseparable from disability" (235), but more specifically moves on to the "modern" reading that he comes to through Gide's reworking of the legend in his play—"that genius and disease, like strength and mutilation, may be inextricably bound up together." Gide, he remarks, "like the hero of the play, stood at an angle to the morality of society and defended [his] position with stubbornness" (237).

It is finally, I think, these intertwined figures of the wound and the bow, and a stubbornness born of that doubled difference, that we might most usefully retain for now. For through their somatic insistence, they mark off the grounds and the position of a necessary resistance to the warriors—"the normal man"—of a very old world.

Coda: Island Fantasia

This mini-narrative continues the discussion of the "politics of insularity." It's about the island of Manhattan which is also my home: I'm a "native." I offer this mise en abyme as yet another way of thinking about the construction of difference—difference as construction—and about the ways in which the making of islands, literally or metaphorically, seen as a self-conscious gesture of positioning can serve as an ironic comment on identity politics.

The headline to an article in the New York Times *early in February 1989 caught my eye as I was writing "Philoctetes": "Central Park Could Get a Little Island Unto Itself." The article tells of a plan to create an island on an eleven-acre lake in the northeast corner of Central Park. Henry J. Stern, the Parks and Recreation Commissioner, explained his idea: "Manhattan is too large to see at once. I wanted an island you could see from the ground and get a sense of its insularity. Why shouldn't Manhattan have something on that scale—delicate, with the land pushing through the water?"*

The Landmarks Preservation Commission voted favorably on the project, and its vice chairman remarked before they went into session: "It occurs to me that, in the words of Joyce Kilmer, 'only God can make a tree.' If we pass the motion on the table, maybe someone will say, 'But commissions can make an island.'"

NOTES

I am grateful to Susan Stanford Friedman for inviting me to the "Conference on Narrative Literature" which she organized—with great critical tact—at Madison, Wisconsin, in April 1989. Because I believe occasional writing is important and to be encouraged as a mode of political intervention, I regret not having been able to publish the essay as part of the conference proceedings in the *Journal of Narrative Technique* (Spring 1990) that Susan Stanford Friedman edited.

I would also like to thank Rosi Braidotti for bringing me back to Utrecht, and the students in Comparative Literature at Yale University—especially Robert Livingston—for the chance to present "Philoctetes" in the context of the lecture series dedicated to the memory of Julia Dahl and Birgit Baldwin.

1. The book, including this essay, appeared in 1989. The page references are from the book version.

Although I've consulted several Woolf scholars, I've been unable to locate this quotation, and have begun to wonder whether it's been misremembered. Just as the critic converts my phrase "women's writing" to "gender difference," is this a transformation of: "it is fatal for any one who writes to think of their sex" (108)? Woolf, moreover, tends to use the word sex, not gender, to mark constructed gendered identities.

2. The Donoghue piece, "A Criticism of One's Own," originally appeared in the *New Republic* and was reprinted in *Men in Feminism*, where I commented on its rhetorical strategies.

3. Other examples that come to mind include Richard Levin's "reading" of feminist Shakespeareans in the pages of *PMLA* and Jeffrey Hart's "Wimmin Against Literature" in the *National Review* (which also uses Woolf—Mrs. Woolf—against the "feminist professors" and enlists the "it is fatal for anyone who writes to think of their sex" against their analyses [44]). Most recently we have Helen Vendler's "Feminism and Literature" that appeared in the *New York Review of Books*.

I should also say for the record that my own feminist criticism, in the form of the essay "Emphasis Added," comes briefly under (unfriendly) scrutiny in this overview. On the occasion of the conference at Madison, I included a discussion of those remarks, with what I hoped sounded like a certain contempt, which I enjoyed reading aloud to a sympathetic audience. It has seemed to me, however, in the time that has elapsed since that event that the emphasis I want to place in this version of the essay falls less on me— nothing personal—than on the more general rage against feminist theory and practice.

4. On this matter, we may well consult the great moralist Trollope, who offers these austere views of the practice in *The Duke's Children* (the conversation is between the Duke and his younger son Gerald about his acquaintance, "a so-called gentleman"):

"He should know black from white. It is considered terrible to cheat at cards."

"There was nothing of that, sir."

"The man who plays and cheats has fallen low indeed."

"I understand that, sir." (517)

5. I owe the image of your "average feminist critic [as the] helpless victim of dangerous lesbian hijackers" to Maaike Meijer, who wonders, sardonically, about Shaw's contradictory defense of "the moral need for an artistic space, where no such thing as morality exists—the ethics of the unethical."

6. Donoghue writes in the same spirit: "Indeed, feminist criticism seems at its present stage to me to be a libel upon women" (151).

7. In his response to the version of this chapter that I read at the "Conference on Narrative Literature," D.A. Miller commented, with an edge of misgiving, on the degree to which its writing "finds its source and support in self-vindication . . . shielding the author's very body against (real, remembered, imagined) attack." Perhaps.

8. I am quoting here from the text of the Director's public remarks, which at my request he communicated to me in written form at the close of the school's meeting.

9. In the February 6, 1989, issue of the *Nation*, in an exchange of letters, Kors complains about being misquoted.

10. Michael Awkward provides an evenhanded discussion of this complicated issue—do you have to be black to read a black-authored text, etc.—via the work of Clifford Geertz, notably the essay " 'From the Native's Point of View,'" in his article "Race, Gender, and the Politics of Reading."

It is worth observing, as a participant at the conference on narrative pointed out in the question period, that in the first case, FC is seen as foreign—influenced by France, using recherché words; here, native. In both, FC is marked off as different from a transparent, essentialized self-identity: Art, Literature, The Critic, The Text, etc.

11. A good summary can be found in P.E. Easterling's "*Philoctetes* and Modern Criticism."

12. The Lemnian setting, it should be mentioned, "was traditionally associated [both] with the Cybele cult and with myths that center on murderous conflict between men and women or exclusive occupancy of the island by women." Indeed, the "most famous myth is that of the Lemnian women killing all the men on the island in revenge for desertion." It is also possible, following out this connection, to interpret, as some scholars have, the "offensive odor of the mythic Lemnian women" as transposed "in Philoctetes's foul wound" (Greengard, 47–48).

13. But like Philoctetes, our difference—according to the legend—is marked in our bodies.

14. In April 1990, I gave a version of this paper at the "Third Annual Conference on Women's Studies" at Dubrovnik. As luck would have it, from my room at the hotel I could see the island of Lokrum, a large beautiful island, thick with trees, which we went to visit one afternoon on a boatride. After contemplating the island for several days, and making the trip there, I realized I had not sufficiently figured in the ambivalence of perspective that double siting creates: the politics of oscillation. (This could also point to another fable about feminism, the referent, and movements of political liberation, but I will have to leave that for another time.) I thank Myriam Diaz-Diacoretz and Nada Popovich for including me in this event.

I am grateful to Seth Schein for taking the time to talk to me about *Philoctetes* (and for introducing me to the work of Carola Greengard). And to David Bady for his pointed reading of an earlier version of this essay.

8

Teaching Autobiography

What I have written strains to be true but
nevertheless is not true *enough*. Truth is anecdotes,
narrative, the snug opaque quotidian.

—John Updike, *Self-Consciousness*

*This essay was written for a conference devoted to the subject of
autobiography. The fact of that focus—the knowledge that the participants in the event and the audience were already convinced of the
genre's importance (whether autobiography should be defined as a
genre is of course another matter)—seems to have authorized me (in a
reflection here about self-authorization) to go further in the mode I'm
calling narrative criticism than I had been willing to go before. Writing
autobiographically about autobiography—which is less common than
one might imagine—also led me (before the fact) to include the occasion
as biographeme in the structure of the writing.*

*At the conference itself there was something exhilarating in the
effects of a common frame of reference that by its very nature was both
constructed and embodied. And there was something irresistible for
me in the chance to write for a context in which it was not necessary
to prepare the ground (as is the case in this book, say, for "Getting
Personal") before advancing. Nonetheless, rereading it now well after
the fact, I see that the essay still struggles defensively with the problems
left unsolved in "Dreaming, Dancing": the waltz of the "as a"s; the
obligatory dance cards of representativity—even, or perhaps especially,
at the heart of feminism's self-writing.*

Getting Personal

August 23, 1989.

I'm on leave in Paris. Sitting here, at the end of summer, trying to get back there, to what was I thinking of when I picked the title "Teaching Autobiography." Find the abstract in the computer:

"Teaching Autobiography"

This will be a paper about contemporary (after mid-1970s) U.S. minority, feminist autobiographies—*Woman Warrior, The House on Mango Street, Fierce Attachments,* etc. Specifically, I want to talk about my experience teaching this literature to adult-degree students (primarily women) in a large, urban public university. I'm especially interested in questions of identification: to what extent does reading autobiography require the ability (the desire?) to identify with "the other"? Is a common gender, ethnicity, class location, racial identity, etc. the basis of the connection? Or are certain themes more powerful than location: the struggle with the mother, the desire to become a writer, the need to resist the "maternal" culture, etc.? Is it possible to theorize the reading of autobiography, women's reading of women's autobiography, etc. Is it desirable? I may also consider the current autobiographical mode in feminist criticism as a way of shaping the question of reading and theory.

Yes, well. All true, but how to go about writing such a paper? Do I even *want* to write it? The abstract, whatever excuses one can make for the necessary pretentiousness of the genre, seems to have been produced by a feminist computer: mine is of course responsible, but any number of other feminist computers could have generated it. All the buzzwords are there; the language oozes political correctness while nonetheless falling into the trap of condescension through implicit self-positioning (the worst kind): the first-world, majority "theorist" who will, in the interest of politicizing the field of theory, have recourse to experience: her own, and presumably—through hers—her students. Poor students.

Still, I did teach the course; it was pretty interesting; the students, they said it themselves, "learned a lot," "got a lot out of it," and I've promised to write something on the subject because I got a lot out of it, too. What I got of course is less easy to say than what I think they got.

The difficulty I experience around writing this paper is inseparable from a problem about the language to say it in: saying the right thing, in this instance, about teaching for the first time in a non-elite institution. Anxiety about sounding classist—which positioned as I am here I cannot fail to do—but also at the same time irritation with the language police and impatience with my introjected feminist correctness.

In the spring of 1988, I left Barnard College and Columbia University where I had taught in various capacities for almost twenty years and where I had also done my undergraduate and graduate studies. I left a campus located in walking distance of the apartment in which I had grown up. It would not be putting too fine a point on the matter to say that I was finally leaving home. Home, but not New York, since I was changing institutions but not cities. That's not quite right either. I did change boroughs. The new job at Lehman College required going from Manhattan to the Bronx—almost an hour by subway.

The question I am most often asked about Lehman—especially by New Yorkers from Manhattan like me—is about location: where is it? The question itself is more significant than its answer, because in fact there is no good answer beyond saying: it's in the Bronx. No one who asks the question ever seems to know where anything else in the Bronx is. The Bronx is a place without landmarks for the people who don't live there. There are famous exceptions of course: there's the Bronx Zoo, Yankee Stadium, and Loehmann's. But unless you have small children, love baseball, or shop for bargains you can't return, you will not be helped by these local toponyms. And it would be possible, moreover, to go to any of these places and still not know where they are, except in relation to a subway station. There's Riverdale, of course, which is the Bronx, too; only the nice part near the Hudson River that gets not to call itself the Bronx (and where a new Loehmann's has just opened).

The Bronx is also a place that people "from" Manhattan often come from (as opposed to move to), or once had relatives in. One of my grandmothers lived in the Bronx and I visited her there—but where?—when I was a child. In that sense, the Bronx is a place that historically one leaves, without leaving it behind. The myth of the old Bronx—

a myth of immigrant community: Jewish, Italian, and Irish—is still powerful for New York writers as a scene in which questions of cultural identity and individual autonomy are staged with particular intensity. I'm thinking most recently of the memoirs of life in the old Bronx by two women writers: Kate Simon published the first installment of her autobiography under the title *Bronx Primitive* in 1983, and Vivian Gornick a memoir called *Fierce Attachments* in 1987.

In the spring of 1989 I taught a course I called—expanding on Carolyn Heilbrun's recent book title—"Reading and Writing Women's Lives" to women in an adult-degree program at night. According to the unwritten mandate of the adult-degree program, students were above all to be encouraged to believe that they could undertake and complete a B.A., a process, measured by the accumulation of credits, that might take a dauntingly long number of years. The life time this commitment represented was a fact the women all emphasized during their initial self-presentations. And it is perhaps this perspective (in addition to their age—twenty-eight to sixty-eight) that most radically distinguishes these women from what are called "traditional" students. This difference further complicated for me the already complicated traditional teacher/student relationship between women that I had grown accustomed to at Barnard, where the students, especially over the last few years, had begun to confuse me with their mother (their "mom" as they would say). But outside those familial categories, which I in fact had come to find dangerously immobilizing, how to find the right distance, which is also to say closeness? What structured the relations between me as the teacher and the students at Lehman, it seemed to me finally, was a borough and a generation of classing—my parents went to CUNY. What joined us?

August 26.

When I first began working on autobiography in 1977, it was from an assumption I had not thought to question then: that a woman, reading "as a woman," as we now say, would necessarily identify with another woman—the writer of an autobiography: *as a woman*. In that presumption of a desire for identification, I assumed a move—I even named it portentously a dialectics—of connection of woman to woman, a textual bonding between women as reading and writing subjects. Although I had taken some precautions in my generalizations about autobiography—I was talking, I said, about *French* female auto-biographers—my effort to elaborate a poetics of gender difference did not even include an attention to national differences within the category "woman."

To a great extent, this assumption of a universal female subject was of course a sign of the times. Those of us for whom "Is Female to Male as Nature Is to Culture?" or "The Traffic in Women" and other stirring pieces of feminist theory published in the extraordinary years of the 1970s had been apocalyptically illuminating, found it hard to resist the appeal of the monolith. Challenging the universality of the male autobiographical subject—the universal, but as it turned out Western, European, heterosexual, in a word, canonical "I"—seemed an all-consuming task; the Female Subject was his counterpart and adversary. To be sure, by the end of the decade feminist anthropologists were doing cross-cultural work, and decrying the abuses of Feminist Woman. But their appeal for a discourse articulating the diversity of situated, delineated, unevenly developed female subjects was not to find an echo in mainstream feminist literary studies for a while.

In 1989, and I would say, datably at least since 1985 (we could argue about dates), it has become fashionable to be in one's critical language acutely self-conscious about making claims for the woman writer, women's writing; specific acknowledgment about race, class, ethnicity, geography, sexuality, as modes of being in the world that inflect a gendered identity in ways too important to ignore is now an obligatory gesture; sometimes it is more than that.[1] And so thinking about autobiography, post-1985, as a "as a"—white, heterosexual, first-world, middle-class, etc. woman—it is not surprising that I would construct a syllabus along the lines I describe in the abstract. Problema-tizing, as the phrase goes, female identity.

But as the semester wore on, confronted by specifically female structures of writing identity: the elaboration in the autobiographies of the figure of the writer as her mother's daughter—Maxine Hong Kingston's *Woman Warrior* is perhaps the best-known example of this phenomenon (Harriet Jacobs's *Incidents in the Life of a Slave Girl* is a powerful example of a less common positioning, the writer as mother, but also as granddaughter): I felt myself lured back to the zones of the Female Subject.[2]

Is this to argue that women's autobiographical writing "transcends" the specific cultural codes in which it finds expression, which would be the feminist variant of the humanist claim that autobiography is universal? Saint Augustine as Everyman replaced by Margery Kempe, mystic and housewife, as one of my colleagues at Lehman has dubbed her. Rather, following de Lauretis's well-known formulation that the female subject is "en-gendered across multiple representations of class, race, language, and social relations" (*Feminist Studies,* 14), my notion of specificity emerges from a reading for the places in the writing where the female (I really mean to say feminist) autobiographer constructs herself in language—precisely at the intersection of cultural codes about women: the uncontested discourse of first uncle in *Woman Warrior,* for instance, "Girls are maggots in the rice." What are the effects of this construction on the reader—the feminist reader? These at least doubly coded spaces of constructed identity in writing are, I think, what allows for readerly connection across the grain of cultural difference, crossing but not dissolving in a double movement of identification and resistance.

I am not suggesting, therefore, that we can or need to choose one or the other, between Woman and women. But instead, in by now canonical feminist fashion, that we see both at once, allowing for an intermittence of insistence, a textually shifting emphasis. Nonetheless, the emphasis I want to retain here is the shaping force of gender within the social field of writing. In a classroom, where difference is embodied, where moreover women have come together to read "as women"— taking a course "on" women—the *design* of a life shaped by gender and a resistance to its rules tend to reconfigure cultural specificities (this has a lot to do, I think, with the appeal of *Jane Eyre,* but I'm getting ahead of myself).

Let me displace this point, personally, to return to my own "reading as a woman." A couple of years ago, when I was reading over my essay on French women's autobiography for inclusion in my book on women's writing, I suddenly realized, or maybe only admitted I had realized all along, that there was an identification for me in my relation to the autobiographies I had chosen (as was the case with the novels) and this had to do not with their Frenchness, but with the emphasis on the story of the "coming to writing"; coming to writing and at the same time, with the exception of Sand (and her difference is important) the bracketing of the authors' own maternal function. Taken together, the texts of Sand, Stern, Beauvoir, and Colette produce the portrait of a female intellectual and a writer who is either not at all, or not predominantly in her own imaginary, a mother. (For these writers, the secondariness of maternity was in itself a form of cultural resistance.[3])

Looking back, it seems to me that I was quite blind to those grounds for my first attraction to autobiography. So too, the insights of my early work were a function of that very blindness. The first woman's autobiography I read, perhaps of any kind, was probably *Memoirs of a Dutiful Daughter*; and I was definitely that. I was also, like many women of the sixties who were to become feminists of the seventies, struck by the forceful opposition Beauvoir saw for herself between the baby and the book, and by her violent distaste for the dailiness of domestic life.[4]

So if it's true, which I think it is, that what I was finding in those earlier French texts was a way of imagining an adult female identity as a writer (and not a mother), what am I working out with these contemporary American texts? The same thing, no doubt. But with the difference today that I have taken on the task of teaching them, in this case to other women; perhaps as a way to understand how to read them.

How to talk about this?

August 30.

I open the program for the conference at random, casting about hopefully for inspiration, and see the question: "Why Is There No Class in Women's Autobiography?" This is in a session called "Bourgeois Subjects"; surely a session for me, an exemplary case. The question belongs to Carolyn Kay Steedman and perhaps it's not by chance that her question catches my eye because I have just read her *Landscape for a Good Woman*. In fact, I had considered beginning this reflection with a quotation from the book. The narrative is framed by an episode in which a health worker who has visited her mother's home, presumably on the occasion of the birth of the author's baby sister, declares: "This house isn't fit for a baby." Steedman, who recounts the anecdote in a preface entitled "Death of a Good Woman," comments fiercely:

> I will do everything and anything until the end of my days to stop anyone ever talking to me like that woman talked to my mother. It is in this place, this bare, curtainless bedroom that lies my secret and shameful defiance. I read a woman's book, meet such a woman at a party (a woman now, like me) and think quite deliberately as we talk: we are divided: a hundred years ago I'd have been cleaning your shoes. I know this and you don't (2).

What I most struggled with, and wondered about when I taught this group of students, was precisely the power of that divide and the range of its effects. But from the other side; and knowing it. Knowing also that, at the same time, the divide is unstable: a hundred years ago I would have been a tailor's daughter. What then?

I don't think there is "no class in women's autobiography," if, minus any further context, I understand what that phrase means.[5] If the discussion of class seems absent from current discussions of women's autobiography, the inscription of class is certainly, even insistently, present in many contemporary autobiographical works. In any event, recalling Richard Terdiman's reformulation of the famous Stanley Fish theory/anecdote "Is There a Text in This Class" as "Is There Class in This Class?" we might ask here how, in teaching in a class on women's autobiography, one is also teaching class. If, as Terdiman argues, following Pierre Bourdieu, class is "a mode of vision and of division," if "*in classes we learn to class*" (227), what is the fate of power relations between, for instance, a bourgeois subject/teacher and her students in a non-elite classroom? Not only, how do I resist classing their reading (I'm sure that I don't), but how, as a bourgeois subject and a teacher, I negotiate with my students a working relation to autobiographical narratives that emerge from class and race positions not one's own? How, finally, do they class me? These are questions I put forward awkwardly because I dread the language I find myself obliged to cast them in. It immediately sounds false.

We began with *A Room of One's Own.*
I almost always begin with Woolf in courses dealing with women and literature. By its themes and analysis of the relations between making art and the concrete conditions of its production, *A Room* in a course on reading and writing women's lives is exemplary. In this case, moreover, I was particularly eager to begin with a text that addressed the issue of women and poverty, and the inequities between women and men in matters of education and access to culture. But Woolf's collective, fictional, historical autobiography did not play in the Bronx. This group of women found Woolf too foreign; too—the only word for it—elite. *A Room* came to life, I think, finally when I had dragged it through the rest of the semester: Judith Shakespeare everywhere. But for many of them, there was no pleasure of the text.

Despite the massive, and finally neither uninteresting nor wholly unjustified resistance to *A Room of One's Own,* Louise de Salvo's "A Portrait of the *Puttana* as a Middle-Aged Woolf Scholar" was a big hit (we read not only straight autobiography in the course, but personal essays, poetry, and first-person fiction). It is always difficult to know why certain books work in a course and others don't; impossible to generalize about, moreover, because there are too many variables. But my hunch about the success of the de Salvo essay is that it embodied for the students a desire for self-authorization which also modeled a way to enact its consequences. (There is notably a scene in which de

Salvo makes a connection between watching her deaf child learning painfully to speak and her equally painful struggle to finish her dissertation that the students loved.) De Salvo, writing explicitly as a working-class Italian woman (and a mother of sons), writes at the same time as a scholar who can define herself outside those origins and categories; this doubleness offered a parable of possibility to women also doing something not foreseen for them, and liking it.

If many of these students were put off by the *figure* of Woolf's lecturer and moved by de Salvo's *puttana,* they all loved Jane Eyre, triumphant heroine of a fictional autobiography. But what grounded these reactions is complex: neither purely sociological—class, ethnicity, etc.—nor purely textual, or generic. In Brontë's novel, the students admired the rooftop speech that Woolf laments; they vibrated to the rage in Brontë, in Jane, for entitlement in the world: what women are allowed to claim as their domain of experience. Cast in another set of codes, what I think happened in these reading events is that the students found a language of empowerment for themselves—as women. In this sense, I would argue, reading *as women* and feminists, in a highly psychologized take on this dazzling fiction of female self-realization, they cut across, while reading through, the social and cultural specificities of—let's call it in shorthand—the Bronx. We could also say they read as feminist critics, Gilbert and Gubar avant la lettre, recognizing in Brontë's story the autobiography of generations of women whose desires had been transformed into fiction.

August 31.

A while ago I read a call for papers for a volume of personal essays on "the making of feminist scholarship." The editors warn the potential contributors that there will be "no room for untheorized narrative or the merely personal anecdote." The stringency of their language haunts me as I write this piece. How can you tell the difference between the merely personal and the theoretically acute? What are the grounds for establishing the difference? Who decides?

For instance. Since I wrote the last segment of the paper, it's been arranged for me to spend three weeks in Brazil after the conference, lecturing and doing seminars on women and literature, on feminist criticism. This excites and distracts me. I suppose talking about this could be what they meant by merely personal anecdote. But let's take a more postmodern view. As the author of this paper, I also know what's coming next, Gloria Anzaldúa's "Speaking in Tongues: A Letter to Third World Women Writers." So if I leave in the anecdote about going to Brazil here, it both gives me a thematic transition and lets me make the argument through narrative . . .

September 1.

In the official U.S. government materials sent to prepare me for my trip to Brazil I read this sentence in a description of life in Brasilia, one of the three cities in which I will be working: "Servants are necessary."[6]

The passage below from Anzaldúa's essay, which deals with questions of women and entitlement, is also the bridge to my discussion of writing in the context of a course on autobiography:

> Who gave us permission to perform the act of writing? Why does writing seem so unnatural for me? I'll do anything to postpone it—empty the trash, answer the telephone. The voice recurs in me: *Who am I, a poor Chicanita from the sticks, to think I could write?* How dared I even consider becoming a writer as I stooped over the tomato fields bending, bending under the hot sun, hands broadened and calloused, not fit to hold the quill, numbed into an animal stupor by the heat.
>
> How hard it is for us to *think* we can choose to become writers, much less *feel* and *believe* that we can. What have we to contribute, to give? Our own expectations condition us. Does not our class, our culture as well as the white man tell us writing is not for women such as us?
>
> The white man speaks: *Perhaps if you scrape the dark off of your face. Maybe if you bleach your bones. Stop speaking in tongues, stop writing left-handed. Don't cultivate your colored skins nor tongues of fire if you want to make it in a right-handed world* (166).

In a course on feminist theory, I would juxtapose Anzaldúa's prose to Hélène Cixous's rhetoric in "The Laugh of the Medusa" where Cixous, speaking now famously from the place of high Continental theory, exhorts her female readers: "Write! Writing is for you . . . I know why you haven't written . . . Because writing is at once too high, too great for you, it's reserved for the great—that is for 'great men'; and it's 'silly' " (246). When Cixous rebels against the male theorists' vision of women as the "dark continent," a topography in psychoanalytic terms constructed on lack, do her metaphors join or erase Anzaldúa's record of work and physical oppression?

Let's go back briefly to the issue of self-authorization, the permission to write. To be sure, a world of material and symbolic difference separates the histories of these two writers, Anzaldúa and Cixous: they come from different places, as we used to say. At the same time, to the extent that the history of women's writing is also a history of a same reiterated struggle in the face of institutionalized exclusions based on gender, to appropriate language and to rework one's place in its turns, it seems to me that it is precisely at this place of common struggle that women's autobiography takes root. I locate here the site of my own doubts of self-authorization, my own longing for permission to write: going public with private desires. And here, perhaps, we should also be more careful: isn't, for instance, postponing writing by emptying the trash or answering the telephone a strategy of avoidance that cuts across the divide of class (not to say gender) lines? Have I been doing anything else in trying to write this essay?

This returns us to the question of where in autobiographical writing to place the emphasis: the culture in the woman or the woman in the culture. As de Lauretis has widely argued, in imagining the construction of feminist subjects, the future of their difference, the goal is not to try to determine competitively, self-righteously, however ringingly, what is more constraining, or excluding, race, class, sexual preference, or gender; or in what combination. It is neither useful nor really interesting finally to decide who had the most difficulty coming to writing. As Anzaldúa, later in the essay, says with some impatience: "Forget the room of one's own—write in the kitchen, lock yourself up in the bathroom" (170). Rather, coming back now to the question of identity pedagogy, to the extent that in a course on autobiography, in which women, who like Anzaldúa's and Cixous's rhetorical sisters, find it hard to believe that writing is *for them,* the question becomes how to find a way to answer the letter. In the classroom, the issues of permission and self-authorization present themselves with another, practical, and material emphasis: discovering a parable of possibility.

I am not a teacher of writing, but I was asked to have the students write. And then, having asked them to write, and announced that I was not a writing teacher, corrected their writing. And performed my part as a force for anti-writing in Anzaldúa's script. About teachers and correction, she writes: "The schools we attended or didn't attend did not give us the skills for writing nor the confidence that we were correct in using our class and ethnic languages. I, for one, became adept at, and majored in English to spite, to show up, the arrogant racist teachers who thought all Chicano children were dumb and dirty" (165–66). I found myself one day, having taught the Anzaldúa essay, returning a set of papers, most of them scrawled over in the margins with *awk, diction, tone, sentence structure,* etc. Seeing myself in their eyes as that teacher, I could not fail to point out my enactment of the role; they nodded with a certain jubilation. But that of course did not solve the writing problem.

Was it absolutely necessary to insist upon "critical writing" in a course on autobiography? For whom *is* critical writing produced, besides for us and graduate students wanting to replace us? And to what end? So, on the assumption that the main thing was to write something, instead of a second critical essay I assigned the writing of what I called "autobiographical fragments." My notion in asking for short takes of personal experience was to bypass both the problem of institutional writing, with its canonized standards of correctness, and the plot of becoming that characterizes canonical autobiography. I wanted a short text, two to three pages, that would be read aloud—and to ask for an emblematic episode within those constraints seemed unfair, although, as it turned out, not undoable. To reduce the panic level the assignment of self-representation raised in some of the students, I suggested the mode of self-portrayal through the portrait of another (they had the examples of Colette's portraits of her father, and the characters of *The*

House on Mango Street). This was the solution most of the students chose.

I want to describe briefly two of the pieces written that spring to evoke some of the drama of what happened with this writing experiment. By what happened I mean more specifically the language through which these students—many of whom had to struggle with themselves to return to school in the first place—found a way to construct some form of public self-representation: through writing.

The first example, which in fact was the first piece read in the class, was ominously entitled "Letter to My Unborn Children." In the seconds that elapsed between the announcement of the title and the actual reading of the essay I panicked internally and regretted I had so quickly given up on compare and contrast. The student, a woman in her late thirties, was as far as I knew, the only gay woman in the group, and I wondered whether this was going to be the occasion of a coming out, or maybe an account of abortions, or both. I was more worried about a coming out because hints of a generalized homophobia had from time to time punctuated class discussion. Instead we heard an articulate account explaining why a woman, looking back on her life, felt that the other things she had wanted for herself did not seem to include a context in which to have children; that it wasn't that she hadn't wanted children or that she wouldn't have loved them—sufficiently imagined to be the addressees of this text—rather, that she hadn't seen how to do this, and that now it was too late; she lacked the energy, and, she thought, had become too selfish. The class listened in awed silence and finally burst into applause (also into tears). I felt that she had in some ways told my story, but at the same time that I couldn't say anything because "I was the teacher." I had decided I had to remain publicly as neutral as possible: not to reward someone's life, especially if it resembled my own, with pedagogic approval, not to say a good grade.

The second instance was the portrait of a greatly beloved grandmother by a mother in her mid-thirties. When she read the last line of her text which came to conclude her feelings for this grandmother—"I wish she had been my mother"—she choked, and, as though horrified by her own words, apologized to the class, trying to take them back. By this time, we were all fishing around in our purses for handkerchiefs.

Not all of the pieces of course were successful; nor were they all poignantly delivered; some were ironic and funny; some were solemn, conventional and fell a little flat. But these students—*almost* all of them—could write; they heard it in each other, and in themselves. I would never have known this if I had kept on assigning conventional paper topics; they might never have known it, either.

At the end of the semester, when we were reviewing the course, the author of the portrait of the grandmother said she wanted to say two things: the first, that what she had learned in the course was that it was OK to have mixed feelings about your mother (my own mother would not have been surprised to learn that this was the net effect of my teaching!); and the second that her boss had given her a desk calendar and that she had begun writing something in it—something for herself—every day.

What I come back to as I try to locate the specific point of *teaching* autobiography—as a social and institutional activity distinct from merely reading autobiography or theorizing it—is that teaching autobiography provides texts for reading that engender the coming to writing in others. Perhaps the essence of autobiography as a genre—or rather one of its most valuable effects—is to enable this process. To say this is also to say that autobiography in its *performance as text* complicates the meaning and reading of social identity, and hence of the writing subject.

September 3.

The day before Labor Day and I see on my American calendar a slightly dowdy female figure, drawn by Roz Chast, my favorite *New Yorker* cartoonist, standing in the countryside, wearing a pair of shorts and wondering with an air of pursed bewilderment: "Where has Summer gone?"

Here it already feels like autumn; I'm wearing a sweater, and feeling glad not to be returning to teaching. I'm not sure I really enjoy teaching,

even when I can give myself (and others) a self-congratulatory account
of it. Teaching makes me anxious and teaching autobiography is no exception. I worried all semester, a little like former Mayor Koch: "How
am I doing?" Do they like this? Or are they just jollying me along: telling
me what they are learning that I like to hear? *They know that I want them
to want to write.* How should I be with them? Am I being elitist? Am I
asking them to choose my values? Denying their own? Agonies of self-
positioning: am I othering them? myself? In particular, I also worried, in
a course on women's lives, what to say about my own. Should I have read
a piece of my own autobiographical writing?

My compromise in self-revelation was to teach, probably with more
feeling than critical distance, a book I have come to think of as "my"
autobiography—its "I" is New York, Jewish, middle-aged, intellectual,
difficult, etc.—*Fierce Attachments.* And by way of shaping a conclusion
to this reflection, I want to describe my sense of personal connection
with the work *as writing;* and what the effects of this hyper-identifica-
tion might have to add to a discussion of understanding the experience
of reading and teaching autobiography.

I should say first that the ways in which, according to the checkpoints
of locational identity, I am like her are also ways in which I'm not like
her at all: I am not the daughter, but the granddaughter of Jewish
immigrants; we were not working-class but middle-class; I grew up in
Manhattan, not the Bronx; there was no erotic female figure like Nettie
in my life; my father didn't die when I was young; I didn't have a
brother but a sister, etc. And yet despite these important differences, I
felt written by this book. The place of identification for me, or rather
the point of entry into the deepest rhythms of the text, was in the
particular intensity of the relationship to the mother, a long, violent,
and ongoing war, though perhaps evolving at the end into a more
complex and productive antagonism.

Labor Day.

Rebecca Hogan, who is leading a discussion section on teaching
autobiography at the conference, has written to ask if she can circulate

my paper to the panelists. I'm wondering whether I can finish writing in time to do this, and whether the paper at this point can take the kind of scrutiny she has in mind; she is nice about letting me say no, but that doesn't make my decision any easier. For now, I should just try to finish.

I don't know how to talk about *Fierce Attachments*. I feel too close to this book—I'm sure I taught it badly—and I don't know how to render its power for me now. The memoir is structured by an intersection of present and past, and the bridging material that holds these temporalities together is a series of fraught exchanges between the mother and daughter that take place as they walk the streets of Manhattan; but the text ends on a scene of immobility; a conversation held on a hot night in August. The apartment has air conditioning, but the two women, who love "real air," open the window wide, and the last exchange of the memoir is set against the blank protection of that New York noise:

> She is lying stretched out on the couch, her arm across her forehead. I sink down into a chair not far from the couch. This couch and this chair are positioned as they were in the living room in the Bronx. It is not difficult to feel that she has been lying on this couch and I have been sitting in this chair almost the whole of our lives.
>
> We are silent. Because we are silent the noise of the street is more compelling. It reminds me that we are not in the Bronx, we are in Manhattan: the journey has been more than a series of subway stops for each of us. Yet tonight this room is so like that other room, and the light, the failing summer light, suddenly it seems a blurred version of that other pale light, the one falling on us in the foyer.
>
> My mother breaks the silence. In a voice remarkably free of emotion— a voice detached, curious, only wanting information—she says to me, "Why don't you go already? Why don't you walk away from my life? I'm not stopping you."
>
> I see the light, I hear the street. I'm half in, half out. "I know you're not, Ma" (204).

We talked in class about the meaning of the journey, now a familiar trope for these students, especially since *Jane Eyre* and *Incidents in the Life of a Slave Girl*. We talked about the difference between changing

Lispector's amuar cockroach

scenes and changing. And we compared the figure of the daughter's ambivalence—half in, half out—to the daughter of *The Woman Warrior,* who had to get out of "hating range" in order to write herself out of silence. In other words, we did everything but ask the question to which the answer belongs probably neither in the classroom, nor in an academic paper. The answer to the mother's question: "Why don't you go already?"

September 5.

I've written myself into a bind: like the daughter in the hot room, listening to the noise of the street: half in, half out. I don't want to end "theoretically" in a piece so grounded in the accidents of practice. I probably should do more with this slightly reworked (I had typed: reworded) concept of identification, bring in Nancy Chodorow, for instance; with class in the (Women's Studies) classroom, but it doesn't seem worth it (I also think it's been done).[7] I don't want to add further to the wonderful set of commonplaces about autobiography we all already trade in (I will leave the task to the younger and more aerobic). Maybe dealing with autobiography binds one irretrievably to the common place. Maybe that's the whole point.

I would rather end personally, but I'm afraid to go too far, though it may be worse not to go far enough: what does a woman, no longer a daughter, who does not enter the maternal, turn into?

What remains, I think, is to give the last word, or almost, to the autobiography that made me want to teach autobiography, and also to write one. This is a passage that was widely excerpted when *Fierce Attachments* was published:

> We became, my mother and I, all women conditioned by loss, unnerved by lassitude, bound together in pity and anger. After Hiroshima dead bodies were found of people who had been wearing printed kimonos when they were killed. The bomb had melted the cloth on their bodies, but the design on the kimonos remained imprinted in the flesh. It seemed to me in later years the deep nerveless passivity of that time together had become the design burned into my skin while the cloth of my own experience melted away (128).

138

Perhaps the question of teaching autobiography remains precisely the task of negotiating in the public space of the classroom what remains, must remain unsaid and most intensely private—the unanswered question of another's life: "Why don't you go already?" The task of teaching autobiography, we know, like the reading of it, entails learning to make out the texture of one's own experience—one's own blank, suffering immobility—beneath the other's imprint; in order to walk away and move on; but to do this requires first recognizing the radical separateness of the other's design, the sound of another's voice; to do this in the classroom may require writing it down for the others to hear.

Separateness, but not fixed in otherness: a sustained and self-consciously performed oscillation between the two, as between two distinct places, like Manhattan and the Bronx, an island and a mainland that are no less connected by the dirt and noise of public transportation. To produce this in the classroom demands an almost impossible tact.

By now it must be clear that I have been turning around another quotation in my effort to find a place to stop. It is the last line from Luce Irigaray's violent first-person, perhaps autobiographical, daughter/mother dialogue, "And the One Doesn't Stir Without the Other": "And what I wanted from you, Mother, was this: that in giving me life, you still remain alive" (67).[8]

I will end here for now.

Coda: Loehmann's, Or, Shopping with My Mother

The old Loehmann's at Jerome Avenue and 183rd Street closed its doors at the end of my first semester at Lehman. I knew this was going to happen—it had been reported in the New York Times *as another sign of the old Bronx's demise—and I planned a special trip there when classes were over: a pilgrimage to the site of archaic female bonding rituals. The sight alone of women's bodies of all ages in various stages* and styles of undress parading about in front of the mirrors in the common changing rooms—asking for and getting advice: "it's not you," "it doesn't do anything for you"—marked one for life. (I was especially fascinated by the shapes of the older women—encased in pantyhose, and packed into elaborately structured bras and girdles of another era—trying on velvet, sequined, and laméd dresses for what were referred to, as if in code, as "functions.")

I hadn't been to the store for many years—I had shopped there with my mother fairly often in the early seventies—and I was hoping to have a Proustian experience when I hit the racks: an intense, physical recovery of those lost moments. I was also, of course, hoping to "get something" (in shopping discourse). In that sense, I did very well, as we used to say. I bought a coat for $49 (!) and a great pair of (lined, of course) wool pants with the label cut out. The coat even had that original detail—an attached shawl—that always satisfied my mother's rigorous shopping standards: not for her the "Fords," the coat (or dress) everyone else wore (and that I cravenly desired when I was young). But nothing magical happened. In part this was because Loehmann's wasn't really my mother's store—she preferred Klein's and May's at Union Square where you could return things—in part because the store was already no longer itself. Everyone was talking about the new store, when it would open—across town, in Riverdale. Just talking in terms of "the old store," "the new store"—which was also true of Klein's and May's—makes me feel that I'm writing in my mother's (matronly?) language.

But if my actually going to Loehmann's failed to bring those memories to life, Fierce Attachments contains a scene in a greasy spoon on Third Avenue in which the two women discuss the age-old topic between Jewish generations—what children owe parents—that captured the heart of what going shopping with my mother really meant: having the conversation. Although the conversation Gornick records was instantly familiar—the trump card always being: "Because I'm your mother"—what got to me by its unnerving proximity to my own experience was a detail in the staging of the mother's need (demand is closer to the truth of it) for hot coffee.

Teaching Autobiography

I remembered sitting with my mother after shopping, in one of those Greek-owned coffee shops that women in New York seem to feel drawn to, especially when they're alone. Hunched into the far corner of the booth, rigid with embarrassment (or was it merely resentment?), I would ostentatiously light a cigarette when my mother, like Gornick's, made the waiter come back to our table with a fresh pot of steaming coffee until it satisfied her requirement for "hot" (in which the "t" always carried an extra charge—almost a dentalization, normally repressed, to make the point). Remembering those scenes between my mother and me through the memory of another's mother, it suddenly became clear that what pained me now was not what mattered then: the recourse to maternal entitlement—particularly unfair, I thought, since it looked more and more unlikely that I would be trading roles with a child of my own ("You'll see when you have children"). What I saw now through Gornick's then was my mother's imperious, personal determination to get what she wanted. At least within this circumscribed realm of daily life, she got her hot coffee. And I?

NOTES

I am grateful to Kathleen Ashley for inviting me to "The Subject of Autobiography," a conference held at the University of Southern Maine in September 1989.

1. 1985 was the date of two major feminist conferences, "Feminism/Theory/Politics" (Pembroke Center, Brown University) and "Feminist Studies: Reconstituting Knowledge" (University of Wisconsin-Milwaukee) that addressed these issues head on. It is the closing date of the essays collected in Adrienne Rich's *Blood, Bread, and Poetry*; "Notes for a Politics of Location" is dated 1984, etc. 1985 also saw the publication of several feminist anthologies which also cap a moment of extraordinary development: see "Parables and Politics" in this volume for more detail about these collections.

2. I'm not happy with that formulation. How to show both the interest of breaking down the feminist universal and the dangers (including ridicule) of doing it like the U.N., or painting by numbers. But then in a second stage, return to the question of the Female Subject to consider the ways in which the new diverse and plurally constituted subjects are also women. Put another way, I started out in this second phase thinking that the emphasis on cultural differences not only would but should prevent me from having any "essentialist" notions about women's autobiography, and I wound up wanting to talk about themes and structures specific to women's autobiography: notably as they are

embodied in the writing daughter's relation to her mother, and in the relation of the daughter's writing to maternal discourse and cultural discourse about women.

My sense of the importance of the relation between women's autobiographical figuration and the maternal rejoins the readings articulated in many of the essays collected in the recent volume devoted to women's autobiography, *Life/Lines,* edited by Bella Brodzski and Celeste Schenck.

3. In Sand's life, however, the maternal role was very important to the construction of the persona, as was the whole, complicated family map. It might even be argued that Sand's most successful production turned out to be her familial scenario; and in particular, her final incarnation as the grandmother in her correspondence with Flaubert. On Sand and the art of being a grandmother, see Naomi Schor's forthcoming "George Sand and the Novel of Idealism."

4. Julia Kristeva's recent autobiographical fiction which she called, intertextually, *Les Samouraïs* (Paris: Fayard, 1990) in direct counterpoint to Beauvoir's *The Mandarins,* marks a deliberate postfeminist difference to that moment in feminist history committed to the demystification—and deferral—of maternity. The last section is called "Maternité" and is a lyrical representation of the mystical pleasures of pregnancy, birth, and motherhood.

5. Steedman did not come to the conference, and so I don't know how she would have glossed her title.

6. As it turned out, most of the women I met—middle-class academics like me— employed servants who lived with them, cared for their children, and took care of their houses. This was perhaps the single point that most feminists I spoke to identified as *the* problem within Brazilian feminism, and the place of contradiction in their own lives.

7. Susan Stanford Friedman has used Chodorow's work productively in her illuminating essay "Women's Autobiographical Selves: Theory and Practice."

8. The French reads: "Et ce que j'attendais de toi, c'est que, me laissant naître, tu demeures aussi vivante."

9

My Father's Penis

When I was growing up, my father wore what we used to call string pajamas. Actually, I only remember the bottom part of the pajamas, which as their name might suggest, tied with a string at the waist. (On top he wore a ribbed sleeveless undershirt that tucked into the pajama bottoms.) The pajamas, made of a thin cotton fabric, usually a shade of washed-out blue, but sometimes also striped, were a droopy affair; they tended to bag at the knees and shift position at the waist with every movement. The string, meant to hold the pajamas up, was also meant to keep the fly—just a slit opening in the front—closed. But the fly, we might say modernly, resisted closure and defined itself instead by the meaningful hint of a gap.

As my father wandered through the apartment in the early mornings, performing his domestic rituals (bringing my mother her coffee in bed, making my sister and me breakfast in the kitchen, shaving, watering the plants), this almost gap never failed to catch my eye. It seemed to me as I watched him cheerfully rescue the burning toast and pass from room to room in a slow motion of characteristic aimlessness (memorialized in our family codes by the Yiddish trope of *draying*), that behind the flap lay something important: dark, maybe verging on purple, probably soft and floppy. I also suspected it was hairy in there; I was pretty sure I had glimpsed hair (he had hair everywhere, on his back and shoulders, why not there).

I don't think I wanted to see it—"it" had no name in my ruminations—but there was a peculiar way in which its mysterious daily existence behind the slit in the pajama bottoms loomed large in my prepubescent imaginary as somehow connected to the constant tension in our family, especially to my mother's bad moods. Growing up, I had only the vaguest notions of sex; I can still remember my utter astonishment when, sitting on the living room couch and feeling vastly sophisticated, I learned from my mother that a penis had to become "erect" to enter a vagina (I had never really thought about *how* the *man's* penis—in the redundant but always less than instructive language of hygiene classes—gets into the *woman's* vagina). So that several years later when in college I finally had a look at my first penis (this was no small surprise), I realized that I had never visualized the thing to myself at all.

Almost forty years after the scene of these memories, I find myself again, as a middle-aged, therapized intellectual, thinking about my father's penis. Now, living alone after my mother's death in the same apartment, my father, stricken with Parkinson's disease, shuffles through the room *draying*. Boxer shorts have replaced the string pajamas, but the gap remains the same and it's still dark in there. But it's not the same: I have seen his penis. I have even touched it. One day when his fingers had grown so rigid he couldn't, as he puts it, "snare" his penis, he wanted to get up to go to the bathroom. It was late and I wanted to go home, so looking and looking away, I fished his penis out from behind the fly of his shorts and stuck it in the urinal; it felt soft and a little clammy.

Shirley, the nurse's aide who takes care of my father, reported one day that when she arrived at the apartment in the morning, she had found my father in the kitchen "bare-bottomed" and cold. "His ---- was blue," she said (the cadences of a slight Caribbean accent made the word hard to understand over the phone); "I rubbed it until it turned pink. Then he felt better." Rubbed his *penis*? But what else, in the vicinity of a bare-bottom, of two syllables, could have gone from blue to pink? Did it respond to her rubbing? Become erect? The mystery returns. What do I know? Shirley and I talk about my father, his care. The apartment, despite her efforts, smells of urine. There's no missing this penis-effect. One day, in the middle of eating dinner, his back to me, he demands his urinal from Shirley, which he uses while at table. Shirley buys him new boxer shorts on 14th Street. Six dollars, she says. Apiece, I ask? No, three Fruit of the Loom in a package.

This is the condition of his remaining at home (he gives me a pained look at the mention of going to a "home" that silences me): to get out of bed and make it to the bathroom without falling, or to use the urinal that hangs like a limp penis from the walker he despises (he shows his superiority to his infirmity by carrying the walker in front of him instead of leaning on it). When these solutions fail, Ellen, the neighbor who brings him his daily *New York Times*, says "he peed himself" (my father always talks more elaborately about the "difficulty of urination," of responding in time to the "urgency of its call"). The newspapers now, like the *New Yorkers* to which he maintains his subscription, and which remain unopened in their plastic wrappers, pile up unread in the living room; I throw them away in my weekly sweep through the apartment.

In "Phallus/Penis: Same Difference" (great title) Jane Gallop writes: "The debate over Lacan's and, beyond that, psychoanalysis's value for feminism itself centers on the phallus. Yet the *phallus* is a very complicated notion in Lacan, who distinguishes it from the *penis*. The distinction seems, however, to resist clarification" (125). For a while after touching my father's penis, I went around thinking smugly I would never again confuse penis and phallus, boasting that I had transcended the confusion. Phallus was the way my father could terrify me when I was growing up: throwing me across the room in a blind rage because I had been talking on the phone—endlessly, it's true—when the hospital called to say his mother was dying; knocking me down in the elevator for staying out late one night with my college boyfriend. Phallus was tearing pages out of the typewriter because I hadn't left wide enough margins on my term papers; making me break a date with the cab driver who had picked me up in London on my first visit there (but Daddy, he's *Jewish*, the son of a cantor!).

Penis was that dark-veined, heavy thing lying there against strangely elongated, even darker balls; hanging between emaciated but still elegant thighs. It made problems for me, but they were finally prosaic, unmediated by concepts and the symbolic order. My father doesn't have the phallus; no one does, Lacan said. But, Gallop writes in *The Daughter's Seduction*, "the need, the desire, the wish for the Phallus is great. No matter how oppressive its reign, it is much more comforting than no one in command" (130–31). So now I decide, say no, and yell; I am responsible for the rest of his life ("it's for your health and welfare," he used to say as his cover for the exercise of an arbitrary authority); maybe I, failing the penis, have my chance at the phallus.

Months after writing this, I come into my father's room. I think I have put an end to all these speculations (penis, phallus, castration, etc.) but when I find him sleeping completely naked, stretched out like an aged Endymion across a hospital bed, I can't resist. His hand is resting in his lap, his penis tucked away out of sight, hidden between his thighs. I move closer.

"So what does it look like?" my sister asks. I don't answer, not only because I want to play big sister one last time, but because I'm not sure I can say what it is that I've seen.

When I wrote "My Father's Penis," I had been thinking more about penises than fathers (or so I thought at the time). Mira Schor, who is a painter and a critic, had done a slide-show lecture on representations of the penis in painting, and I conceived my piece originally as a kind of footnote to her panoply of members—the geriatric extension of her taxonomy. But I was also writing in the aftermath of an intensely charged academic performance in which the status of "experience" in feminist theory had been challenged with a certain phallic—what would a better word be?—insistence. When it then became a matter of publishing "the penis" (it seems impossible to invoke the title or its contents without getting caught in the spiral of catachresis) in *Refiguring the Father*, I felt that I had inadvertently found a destination for it: that the fragmentary essay, because of its mixed origins, born of the troubled intimacies of the autobiographical penis and the theoretical phallus, had unexpectedly come full circle back to feminist revision. But not perhaps back home.

Had my father still been able to read, I would never have written about "the penis." By going public with the details of domestic arrangements on Riverside Drive, I was flying in the face of the parental injunction not to "tell" that had haunted my adolescence and continued well into my adult years; the panic my parents felt that they would be exposed by us; the shame over family secrets. But he was down in his reading to the occasional newspaper headline and, I think, at his end, despite a finely honed personal vanity, beyond caring. He had become no longer himself, and I needed to mourn his disappearance.

My father died before this piece appeared in print. He died, I'm tempted to say, of the penis: at home, as he had wanted, after eating ice cream and watching public television, in the aftermath of a grueling seven-week stay in the hospital that followed a violent urinary tract infection. I dealt with—talked about, looked at, touched, raged at— his penis until the very end. And until the very end, the penis/phallus connection remained alive, impossible to sever. In the hospital, it was war between his penis and the doctors' discourse; or rather my attempt to stand in as phallus for his penis—the rights of his body—against their authority to determine the course of his life; their wish for him to live, against his entire system's disarray (my wish for him?).

When I read one day on my father's chart in the intensive-care unit "Responds only to pain," I found it hard to share the doctor's jubilation over the signs of life dotting the monitor above his respirator. "What do you want me to do," she hissed at me across the network of tubes mapping his body, "kill your father?"

Works Cited

Albright, Ann Cooper. "Incalculable Choreographies." "Mining the Dancefield: Feminist Theory and Contemporary Dance." (ms.)

Anzaldúa, Gloria. "Speaking in Tongues: A Letter to Third World Women Writers." In *This Bridge Called My Back: Writings by Radical Women of Color,* Cherríe Moraga and Gloria Anzaldúa, eds. New York: Kitchen Table: Women of Color Press, 1983.

Ascher, Carole, Louise de Salvo, and Sara Ruddick, eds. *Between Women.* Boston: Beacon Press, 1984.

Awkward, Michael. "Appropriative Gestures: Theory and Afro-American Literary Criticism." In *Gender and Theory: Dialogues on Feminist Criticism,* ed. Linda Kauffman. New York and Oxford: Basil Blackwell, 1989.

———. "Race, Gender, and the Politics of Reading." *Black American Literature Forum* (Spring 1988), 22 (1):5–27.

Barthes, Roland. "La crise du désir." Interview. *Le Nouvel Observateur.* April 20, 1980.

———. *Criticism and Truth.* Trans. Katrine Pilcher Keuneman. Minneapolis: University of Minnesota Press, 1987.

———. "The Death of the Author." In *Image/Music/Text.* Trans. Stephen Heath. New York: Hill and Wang, 1977.

———. *The Pleasure of the Text.* Trans. Richard Miller. New York: Hill and Wang, 1975.

———. *Roland Barthes by Roland Barthes.* Trans. Richard Howard. New York: Hill and Wang, 1977.

———. "Style and its Image." In *Literary Style: A Symposium,* ed. Seymour Chatman. London: Oxford University Press, 1971.

Baudrillard, Jean. *De la séduction.* Paris: Editions Galilée, 1979.

Benjamin, Jessica. "Master and Slave: The Fantasy of Erotic Domination." In *The Powers of Desire: The Politics of Sexuality,* Christine Stansell, Ann Snitow, and Sharon Thompson, eds. New York: Monthly Review Press, 1983.

Berg, Elizabeth L. "Iconoclastic Moments: Reading the *Sonnets for Helene,* Writing the *Portuguese Letters.*" In *The Poetics of Gender,* ed. Nancy K. Miller. New York: Columbia University Press, 1986.

Getting Personal

Bernheimer, Charles. *Flaubert and Kafka: Studies in Psychopoetic Structure*. New Haven: Yale University Press, 1982.

Boone, Joseph. "Of Me(n) and Feminism: Who(se) Is the Sex that Writes?" In *Gender and Theory: Dialogues on Feminist Criticism*, ed. Linda Kauffman. New York and Oxford: Basil Blackwell, 1989.

Bosch, Mineke. "A Woman's Life in a Soapbox." *History Workshop: A Journal of Socialist and Feminist Historians* (Autumn 1987), 24: 166–70.

Bourne, Jenny. "Homelands of the Mind: Jewish Feminism and Identity Politics." *Race and Class* (Summer 1987), 29:1, 1–24.

Brodzki, Bella, and Celeste Schenck, eds. *Life/Lines: Theorizing Women's Autobiography*. Ithaca: Cornell University Press, 1988.

Brownstein, Rachel, M. *Becoming a Heroine: Reading About Women in Novels*. New York: Viking, 1982.

Bruss, Elizabeth W. *Autobiographical Acts: The Changing Situation of a Literary Genre*. Baltimore: The Johns Hopkins University Press, 1976.

Bulkin, Elly and Rena Grasso Patterson. "An Interchange on Feminist Criticism: On 'Dancing Through the Minefield.'" *Feminist Studies* (Fall 1982), 8 (3): 629–75.

Bulkin, Elly, Minnie Bruce Pratt, and Barbara Smith. *Yours in Struggle: Three Perspectives on Anti-Semitism and Racism*. New York: Long Haul Press, 1984.

Carby, Hazel. *Reconstructing Womanhood: The Emergence of the Afro-American Woman Novelist*. New York: Oxford University Press, 1987.

———. "White Woman Listen!: Black Feminism and the Boundaries of Sisterhood." In *The Empire Strikes Back: Race and Racism in 70's Britain*. Center for Contemporary Cultural Studies. London: Unwin Hyman, 1982.

Caws, Mary Ann. *Women of Bloomsbury: Virginia, Vanessa, and Carrington*. New York and London: Routledge, 1990.

Christian, Barbara. "Black Feminist Process: In the Midst of . . ." Introduction. *Black Feminist Criticism*. New York: Pergamon, 1985.

———. "But What Do We Think We're Doing Anyway: The State of Black Feminist Criticism(s) or My Version of a Little Bit of History." In *Changing Our Own Words: Essays on Criticism, Theory, and Writing by Black Women*, ed. Cheryl A. Wall. New Brunswick: Rutgers University Press, 1989.

———. "The Race for Theory." In *Gender and Theory: Dialogues on Feminist Criticism*, ed. Linda Kauffman. New York and Oxford: Basil Blackwell, 1989.

Cixous, Hélène. "The Laugh of the Medusa." Trans. Keith Cohen and Paula Cohen. In *New French Feminisms*, Elaine Marks and Isabelle de Courtivron, eds. New York: Schocken, 1981.

Culler, Jonathan. *On Deconstruction: Theory and Criticism After Structuralism*. Ithaca: Cornell University Press, 1982.

Works Cited

Culley, Margo, and Catherine Portuges, eds. *Gendered Subjects: The Dynamics of Feminist Teaching.* Boston: Routledge and Kegan Paul, 1985.

de Lauretis, Teresa. "Feminist Studies/Critical Studies: Issues, Terms, and Contexts." In *Feminist Studies/Critical Studies*, ed. Teresa de Lauretis. Bloomington: Indiana University Press, 1986.

————. *Technologies of Gender: Essays on Theory, Film, and Fiction.* Bloomington: Indiana University Press, 1987.

Derrida, Jacques, and Christie V. McDonald. "Choreographies." *Diacritics* (Summer 1982), 12 (2): 66–76.

de Salvo, Louise. "Portrait of the *Puttana* as Middle-Aged Woolf Scholar." In *Between Women*, Carole Ascher, Louise de Salvo, Sara Ruddick, eds. Boston: Beacon Press, 1984.

Donoghue, Denis. "A Criticism of One's Own." In *Men in Feminism*, Alice Jardine and Paul Smith, eds. New York and London: Methuen, 1987.

DuPlessis, Rachel Blau. "For the Etruscans." In *The New Feminist Criticism: Women, Literature, and Theory*, ed. Elaine Showalter. New York: Pantheon, 1985.

————. *The Pink Guitar: Writing as Feminist Practice.* Routledge: New York and London, 1990.

Easterling, P.E. "*Philoctetes* and Modern Criticism." *Illinois Classical Studies* (1978), 3: 27–39.

Edelman, Lee. "At Risk in the Sublime: The Politics of Gender and Theory." In *Gender and Theory: Dialogues on Feminist Criticism*, ed. Linda Kauffman. New York and Oxford: Basil Blackwell, 1989.

Eliot, George. *The Mill on the Floss.* New York: Penguin, 1979.

Felski, Rita. *Beyond Feminist Aesthetics.* Cambridge: Harvard University Press, 1989.

Fineman, Joel. "The History of the Anecdote: Fiction and Fiction." In *The New Historicism*, ed. H. Aram Veeser. New York and London: Routledge, 1989.

Fish, Stanley. "Is There a Text in This Class?" *Is There a Text in This Class?: The Authority of Interpretive Communities.* Cambridge: Harvard University Press, 1980.

Foucault, Michel. *The History of Sexuality.* Trans. Robert Hurley. New York: Vintage, 1980.

Friedman, Susan Stanford. "Women's Autobiographical Selves: Theory and Practice." In *The Private Self: The Theory and Practice of Women's Autobiographical Writings*, ed. Shari Benstock. Chapel Hill and London: University of North Carolina Press, 1988.

Fuss, Diana. *Essentially Speaking: Feminism, Nature, and Difference.* New York and London: Routledge, 1989.

Gallop, Jane. *The Daughter's Seduction: Feminism and Psychoanalysis.* Ithaca: Cornell University Press, 1982.

———. "The Perverse Body." *Thinking Through the Body*. New York: Columbia University Press, 1988.

———. "Phallus/Penis: Same Difference." *Thinking Through the Body*. New York: Columbia University Press, 1988.

Gilbert, Sandra M., and Susan Gubar. *The Madwoman in the Attic: The Woman Writer and the Nineteenth-Century Literary Imagination*. New Haven: Yale University Press, 1979.

——— eds. *The Norton Anthology of Literature by Women: The Tradition in English*. New York: W. W. Norton, 1985.

Gilligan, Carol. *In a Different Voice: Psychological Theory and Women's Development*. Cambridge: Harvard University Press, 1982.

Gornick, Vivian. *Fierce Attachments*. New York: Farrar, Straus, Giroux, 1987.

Greenblatt, Stephen. *Renaissance Self-Fashioning*. Chicago: University of Chicago Press, 1980.

Greene, Gayle, and Coppélia Kahn, eds. *Making a Difference*. New York and London: Methuen, 1985.

Greengard, Carola. *Theatre in Crisis: Sophocles' Reconstruction of Genre and Politics in Philoctetes*. Amsterdam: Adolf M. Hakkert, 1987.

Grossman, David. *The Yellow Wind*. Translated from the Hebrew by Haim Watzman. New York: Farrar, Strauss, Giroux, 1988.

Haraway, Donna. "A Manifesto for Cyborgs: Science, Technology, and Socialist Feminism in the 1980s." In *Coming to Terms: Feminism, Theory, Politics,* ed. Elizabeth Weed. New York and London: Routledge, 1989.

Hartsock, Nancy. "Rethinking Modernism: Minority vs. Majority Theories." *Cultural Critique* (Fall 1987), no. 7: 187–206.

Heard, Alex. "Jargonaut." The *New Republic*. January 29, 1990.

Heath, Stephen. "Male Feminism." In *Men in Feminism*, Alice Jardine and Paul Smith, eds. New York and London: Methuen, 1987.

Heilbrun, Carolyn. "Bringing the Spirit Back to English Studies." In *The New Feminist Criticism: Women, Literature, and Theory,* ed. Elaine Showalter. New York: Pantheon, 1985.

———. "Millett's *Sexual Politics*: A Year Later." *Aphra*, 2 (1971): 38–47.

———. "Personal and Prefatory." *Reinventing Womanhood*. New York: W. W. Norton, 1978.

———. *Writing a Woman's Life*. New York: W. W. Norton, 1988.

Hirsch, Marianne. *The Mother/Daughter Plot: Narrative, Psychoanalysis, Feminism*. Bloomington: Indiana University Press, 1990.

Hooks, Bell. *Talking Back: Thinking Feminist, Thinking Black*. Boston: South End Press, 1989.

Works Cited

Hurston, Zora Neale. *Their Eyes Were Watching God.* Urbana and Chicago: University of Illinois Press, 1978.

Irigaray, Luce. "Any Theory of the 'Subject' Has Always Been Appropriated by the 'Masculine.'" *Speculum, of the Other Woman.* Trans. Gillian Gill. Ithaca: Cornell University Press, 1985.

――――. "And the One Doesn't Stir Without the Other." Trans. Hélène Vivienne Wenzel. *Signs* (Autumn 1981), 7 (1): 56–67.

――――. *Et l'une ne bouge pas sans l'autre.* Paris: Minuit, 1979.

Jacobs, Harriet. *Incidents in the Life of a Slave Girl.* In *The Classic Slave Narratives,* ed. Henry Louis Gates, Jr. New York: NAL, 1987.

Jacobus, Mary. "Is There a Woman in This Text?" *Reading Woman: Essays in Feminist Criticism.* New York: Columbia University Press, 1986.

Johnson, Barbara. *The Critical Difference.* Baltimore: The Johns Hopkins University Press, 1980.

――――. "Deconstruction, Feminism, and Pedagogy." *A World of Difference.* Baltimore: The Johns Hopkins University Press, 1987.

――――. "Gender Theory and the Yale School." *A World of Difference.* Baltimore: The Johns Hopkins University Press, 1987.

――――. "Interview" with Imre Salusinszky. In *Criticism and Society,* ed. Imre Salusinszky. London and New York: Methuen, 1987.

Jordan, June. *Civil Wars.* Boston: Beacon Press, 1981.

Kaplan, Alice Y. "Confessions of a Francophile," (ms.)

Kaplan, Cora. *Sea Changes: Essays on Culture and Feminism.* London: Verso, 1986.

Kauffman, Linda, ed. *Gender and Theory: Dialogues on Feminist Criticism.* New York and Oxford: Basil Blackwell, 1989.

Kipnis, Laura. "Feminism: The Political Conscience of Postmodernism?" In *Universal Abandon? The Politics of Postmodernism,* ed. Andrew Ross. Minneapolis: University of Minnesota Press, 1988.

Kolodny, Annette. "A Map for Rereading: Gender and the Interpretation of Literary Texts." In *The New Feminist Criticism: Essays on Women, Literature, and Theory,* ed. Elaine Showalter. New York: Pantheon, 1985.

――――. "Dancing Through the Minefield: Some Observations on the Theory, Practice, and Politics of a Feminist Literary Criticism." In *The New Feminist Criticism: Essays on Women, Literature, and Theory,* ed. Elaine Showalter. New York: Pantheon, 1985.

Kristeva, Julia. *Les Samouraïs.* Paris: Fayard, 1990.

Lejeune, Philippe. *On Autobiography.* Trans. Katherine Leary. Minneapolis: University of Minnesota Press, 1989.

Lentricchia, Frank. "Andiamo!" *Critical Inquiry* (Winter 1988), 14: 407–13.

———. "Patriarchy Against Itself: The Young Manhood of Wallace Stevens." *Critical Inquiry* (Summer 1987), 13: 742–86.

Leonardi, Susan J. "Recipes for Reading: Summer Pasta, Lobster à la Riseholme, and Key Lime Pie." *PMLA* (May 1989), 104 (3): 340–47.

Levin, Richard. "Feminist Thematics and Shakespearean Tragedy." *PMLA* (March 1988), 103 (2): 125–38.

Lipking, Lawrence. "Aristotle's Sister: A Poetics of Abandonment." *Critical Inquiry* (September 1983), 10 (1): 61–82.

Lorde, Audre. "Poetry Is Not a Luxury." *Sister Outsider*. Trumansburg, N.Y.: Crossing Press, 1984.

———. *Zami: A New Spelling of My Name. A Biomythography*. Trumansburg, N.Y.: Crossing Press, 1982.

McDowell, Deborah E. Interview with Susan Fraiman. *Critical Texts: A Review of Theory and Criticism* (1989), 6(3): 13–29.

MacLean, Gerald. "Citing the Subject." In *Gender and Theory: Dialogues on Feminist Criticism*, ed. Linda Kauffman. New York and Oxford: Basil Blackwell, 1989.

Marcus, Jane. "Storming the Toolshed." In *Feminist Theory: A Critique of Ideology*, N. O. Keohane, M. Z. Rosaldo, B. C. Gelpi, eds. Chicago: University of Chicago Press, 1982.

Martin, Biddy. "Lesbian Identity and Autobiographical Difference(s)." In *Life/Lines: Theorizing Women's Autobiography*, Bella Brodzki and Celeste Schenck, eds. Ithaca: Cornell University Press, 1988.

———, and Chandra Mohanty. "Feminist Politics: What's Home Got to Do With It?" In *Feminist Studies/Critical Studies*, ed. Teresa de Lauretis. Bloomington: Indiana University Press, 1986.

Meese, Elizabeth. *Crossing the Double-Cross: The Practice of Feminist Criticism*. Chapel Hill: University of North Carolina Press, 1986.

Messer-Davidow, Ellen. "The Philosophical Bases of Feminist Literary Criticism." In *Gender and Theory: Dialogues on Feminist Criticism*, ed. Linda Kauffman. New York and Oxford: Basil Blackwell, 1989.

Miller, D.A. "*Cage aux folles:* Sensation and Gender in Wilkie Collins's *The Woman in White*." In *Speaking of Gender*, ed. Elaine Showalter. New York and London: Routledge, 1989.

Miller, Nancy K. "Changing the Subject." *Subject to Change: Reading Feminist Writing*. New York: Columbia University Press, 1988. Rpt. in *Coming to Terms: Feminism, Theory, Politics*, ed. Elizabeth Weed. New York: Routledge, 1989.

———. "Man on Feminism." In *Men in Feminism*, Alice Jardine and Paul Smith, eds. New York and London: Methuen, 1987.

Millett, Kate. *Sexual Politics*. New York: Doubleday, 1970.

Works Cited

Moi, Toril. *Sexual/Textual Politics*. London and New York: Methuen, 1985.

Moody, Ann. *Coming of Age in Mississippi*. New York: Dell, 1968.

Moraga, Cherríe. "La Guëra." In *This Bridge Called My Back: Writings by Radical Women of Color*, Cherríe Moraga and Gloria Anzaldúa, eds. New York: Kitchen Table: Women of Color Press, 1983.

———. "The Slow Dance." In *Pleasure and Danger*, ed. Carole S. Vance. Boston: Routledge and Kegan Paul, 1984.

Munich, Adrienne. "Notorious Signs, Feminist Criticism and Literary Tradition." In *Making a Difference*, Gayle Greene and Coppélia Kahn, eds. London and New York: Methuen, 1985.

Nelson, Cary. "Reading Prefaces." *PMLA* (October 1976), 91 (5): 801–15.

Nestle, Joan. *A Restricted Country*. Ithaca: Firebrand Books, 1987.

Olney, James, ed. *Autobiography: Essays Theoretical and Critical*. Princeton: Princeton University Press, 1980.

Orr, Linda. *Headless Histories: Nineteenth-Century French Historiography of the Revolution*. Ithaca: Cornell University Press, 1990.

Ostriker, Alice. "From a New Past to a New Future." Review of Judith Plaskow's *Standing Again at Sinai: Judaism from a Feminist Perspective*. San Francisco: Harper and Row, 1990. The *Women's Review of Books* (September 1990), 7(12): 12.

Pratt, Minnie Bruce. "Identity: Skin Blood Heart." In *Yours in Struggle: Three Perspectives on Anti-Semitism and Racism*. New York: Long Haul Press, 1984.

Presser, Jacques. In *Uit het werk van dr. J. Presser*, ed. M. C. Brands. Amsterdam: Athenaeum Polak & van Gennep, 1979.

Raynaud, Claudine. "'A Nutmeg Nestled Inside Its Covering of Mace': Audre Lorde's *Zami*." In *Life/Lines: Theorizing Women's Autobiography*, Bella Brodzki and Celeste Schenck, eds. Ithaca: Cornell University Press, 1988.

Reagon, Bernice Johnson. "Coalition Politics: Turning the Century." In *Home Girls: A Black Feminist Anthology*, ed. Barbara Smith. New York: Kitchen Table Press, 1984.

Rich, Adrienne. "Notes Toward a Politics of Location." *Blood, Bread, and Poetry: Selected Prose, 1979–1985*. New York: W.W. Norton, 1986.

———. "Vesuvius at Home: The Power of Emily Dickinson." "Taking Women Students Seriously." *On Lies, Secrets, and Silence: Selected Prose, 1966–1978*. New York: W. W. Norton, 1979.

———. "When We Dead Awaken: Writing as Re-vision." *On Lies, Secrets, and Silence: Selected Prose, 1966–1978*. New York: W. W. Norton, 1979.

Riley, Denise. *"Am I That Name?": Feminism and the Category of "Women" in History*. Minneapolis: University of Minnesota Press, 1988.

Robinson, Lillian S. "Treason Our Text: Feminist Challenges to the Literary Canon."

Getting Personal

In *The New Feminist Criticism: Essays on Women, Literature, and Theory*, ed. Elaine
Showalter. New York: Pantheon, 1985.

Russo, Mary. "Female Grotesques: Carnival and Theory." In *Feminist Studies/Critical
Studies*, ed. Teresa de Lauretis. Bloomington: Indiana University Press, 1986.

Ruthven, K.K. *Feminist Literary Studies: An Introduction.* Cambridge: Cambridge University Press, 1984.

Schor, Mira. "Representations of the Penis." *M/E/A/N/I/N/G* (Nov. 1988), No.4: 3–17.

Schor, Naomi. *Breaking the Chain: Women, Theory, and French Realist Fiction.* New
York: Columbia University Press, 1985.

———. "Dreaming Dissymmetry: Barthes, Foucault, and Sexual Difference." In *Men
and Feminism*, Alice Jardine and Paul Smith, eds. New York and London: Methuen,
1987.

———. *Reading in Detail: Aesthetics and the Feminine.* New York and London: Methuen, 1987.

———. "George Sand and the Novel of Idealism" (ms.)

Sedgwick, Eve Kosofsky. *Between Men: English Literature and Male Homosocial Desire.*
New York: Columbia University Press, 1985.

———. "A Poem Is Being Written." *Representations* (Winter 1987), 17: 110–43.

Segrest, Mab. *My Mama's Dead Squirrel: Lesbian Essays on Southern Culture.* Ithaca:
Firebrand Books, 1985.

Shaw, Peter. "Feminist Literary Criticism." *The American Scholar.* Autumn 1988 (495–
513); rpt. in *The War Against the Intellect: Episodes in the Decline of Discourse.*
Iowa City: University of Iowa Press, 1989.

Showalter, Elaine. "Toward a Feminist Poetics." In *The New Feminist Criticism: Essays
on Women, Literature, and Theory*, ed. Elaine Showalter. New York: Pantheon, 1985.

Silver, Brenda, R. "The Authority of Anger: *Three Guineas* as Case Study." *Signs* (Winter
1991), 16 (2): 340–70.

Simon, Kate. *Bronx Primitive.* New York: Harper Colophon, 1983.

Smith, Barbara. "Toward a Black Feminist Criticism." In *The New Feminist Criticism:
Women, Literature, and Theory.* New York: 1985.

Smith, Roberta. "Three Good Arguments for Less Self-Indulgence." The *New York
Times*, September 2, 1990.

Smith, Valerie. *Self-Discovery and Authority in Afro-American Narrative.* Cambridge:
Harvard University Press, 1987.

Snitow, Ann. "Gender Diary." In *Rocking the Ship of State: Toward a Feminist Peace
Politics*, ed. Adrienne Harris and Ynestra King. Boulder: Westview Press, 1989; rpt.
in *Conflicts in Feminism*, Marianne Hirsch and Evelyn Fox Keller, eds. New York and
London: Routledge, 1990.

Works Cited

Spillers, Hortense. "Interstices: A Small Drama of Words." In *Pleasure and Danger*, ed. Carole S. Vance. Boston: Routledge and Kegan Paul, 1984.

Spivak, Gayatri Chakravorty."Finding Feminist Readings: Dante-Yeats." *In Other Worlds: Essays in Cultural Politics*. New York and London: Routledge, 1987.

———. "French Feminism in an International Frame." *Yale French Studies*. "Feminist Readings: French Texts/American Contexts." No. 62, 1981; rpt. *In Other Worlds: Essays in Cultural Politics*. New York and London: Routledge, 1987.

———. "The Political Economy of Women as Seen by a Literary Critic." In *Coming to Terms*, ed. Elizabeth Weed. New York: Routledge, 1989.

Steedman, Carolyn Kay. *Landscape for a Good Woman: A Story of Two Lives*. New Brunswick: Rutgers University Press, 1987.

Sternberg, Janet, ed. *The Writer on Her Work*. New York: W.W. Norton, 1981.

Stimpson, Catharine R. *Where the Meanings Are: Feminism and Cultural Spaces*. New York and London: Methuen, 1988.

Stone, Albert E. *Autobiographical Occasions and Original Acts: Versions of Identity from Henry Adams to Nate Shaw*. Philadelphia: University of Pennsylvania Press, 1982.

Suleiman, Susan R. "(Re)Writing the Body: The Politics and Poetics of Female Eroticism." In *The Female Body in Western Culture: Contemporary Perspectives*, ed. Susan R. Suleiman. Cambridge: Harvard University Press, 1986.

———. "Writing and Motherhood." In *The (M)other Tongue: Essays in Feminist Psychoanalytic Interpretation*, Shirley Nelson Garner, Claire Kahane, Madelon Sprengnether, eds. Ithaca and London: Cornell University Press, 1985.

Terdiman, Richard. "Is There Class in This Class?" In *The New Historicism*, ed. H. Aram Veeser. New York and London: Routledge, 1989.

Tompkins, Jane. "Me and My Shadow." In *Gender and Theory: Dialogues on Feminist Criticism*, ed. Linda Kauffman. New York: Basil Blackwell, 1989.

———. *Sensational Designs: The Cultural Work of American Fiction, 1790–1860*. New York: Oxford University Press, 1985.

Trinh, Minh-ha, T. *Woman, Native, Other: Writing, Postcoloniality and Feminism*. Bloomington: Indiana University Press, 1989.

Trollope, Anthony. *The Duke's Children*. New York: Oxford University Press, 1986.

Walker, Alice. "*One* Child of One's Own." *In Search of Our Mothers' Gardens*. San Diego: Harcourt Brace Jovanovich, 1983.

Weed, Elizabeth, ed. *Coming to Terms: Feminism, Theory, Politics*. New York and London: Routledge, 1989.

Weiner, Jon. "Campus Voices Right and Left." The *Nation*. December 12, 1988: 644–66.

Williams, Patricia. "On Being the Object of Property." In *Feminist Theory in Practice and Process*, Micheline R. Malson, Jean F. O'Barr, Sarah Westphal-Wihl, and Mary Wyer, eds. Chicago: University of Chicago Press, 1989.

Wilson, Edmund. "The Wound and the Bow." *The Wound and the Bow: Seven Studies in Literature*. New York: Oxford University Press, 1965.

Wittig, Monique. "The Mark of Gender." In *The Poetics of Gender*, ed. Nancy K. Miller. New York: Columbia University Press, 1986.

Woolf, Virginia. *A Room of One's Own*. New York: Harcourt, Brace, and World, 1967.

Yaeger, Patricia. *Honey-Mad Women: Emancipatory Strategies in Women's Writing*. New York: Columbia University Press, 1988.

———. "Toward a Female Sublime." In *Gender and Theory: Dialogues on Feminist Criticism*, ed. Linda Kauffman. New York and Oxford: Basil Blackwell, 1989.

———, and Beth Kowaleski-Wallace, eds. *Refiguring the Father: New Feminist Readings of Patriarchy*. Carbondale: Southern Illinois University Press, 1989.

Index

Index

Gender, 20–23, 27n5, 27n8, 28n11, 45, 50–53, 78, 103–106, 107, 108–14; and art, 44; and cultural codes, 126–27; and literariness, 113; and mistakes, 50–52; and spectacle, 22; and violence, xviin8, 23
Gilbert, Sandra M.; 14, *Norton Anthology of Literature by Women,* 57–58, 130
Gilligan, Carol, 28n12
Goldman, Emma, 89
Gornick, Vivian; *Fierce Attachments,* 124, 136–38, 140, 141
Greenblatt, Stephen, 2
Greene, Gayle, 57
Greengard, Carola, 115
Grossman, David, 96
Gubar, Susan; 14, *Norton Anthology of Literature by Women,* 57–58, 130

Haraway, Donna, 75–76
Harris, Rosemary, 46
Hart, Jeffrey, 119n3
Heath, Stephen, xviin7, 2, 21, 26n2, 29n19
Heilbrun, Carolyn, 2, 14, 28n13, 65
Hirsch, Marianne, 3
Hogan, Rebecca, 136–37
Hooks, Bell, 3, 84, 93–94
Humanism, 91, 105, 106, 126
Hurston, Zora Neale; *Their Eyes Were Watching God,* 77, 90

Identity politics, 20, 75–76, 87, 91, 97, 99n8, 118, 124–26, 132. *See also* Experience
Institutions, 47, 66, 68, 71n8, 116
Insularity, 112, 114–17, 118

Irigaray, Luce, 7, 81, 86, 139
Island, 114–17, 118, 120n14
Israel, 96, 100n13

Jacobs, Harriet; *Incidents in the Life of a Slave Girl,* 109–10, 113, 126, 137
Jacobus, Mary, xviin6, 1, 25, 71n9, 75, 104
Jardine, Alice, 18
Jews, 26n4, 95–97, 100n13,14
Johnson, Barbara, 2, 15–16, 17, 87–88
Jordan, June, 3

Kahn, Coppélia, 57
Kaplan, Alice, 3, 48
Kaplan, Cora, 2
Kauffman, Linda, 4
King, Martin Luther, 85, 98–99n6
Kingston, Maxine Hong; *Woman Warrior,* 126, 138
Kipnis, Laura, 20
Kolodny, Annette, 14, 82–83
Kors, Alan, 112, 120n9
Kowaleski-Wallace, Beth, 147n2
Kristeva, Julia, 80, 142n2

LeGuin, Ursula, 11
Lehman College, 123
Lentricchia, Frank, 2
Leonardi, Susan J., 2, 30n24
Lesbian, 84–85, 91–92; and dancing, 81; and homophobia, 134. *See also* Experience
Levin, Richard, 119n3
Lipking, Lawrence, 28n12
Literary criticism, 8–9, 13, 45–47, 106, 111. *See also* Black Feminist criticism; Feminist criticism

Index

Quotation, 93, 94–97, 99n10

Race and racism, xiv, 74, 83, 85,
  86, 108–14, 131. *See also* Black
  feminist criticism
Reader, 8, 29n16, 34–35
Reading, 10, 75, 94–95, 97, 130
Reagon, Bernice, 116–17
Representation, 4, 20, 64, 109
Representativity, ix, x, xii, xiii, 20,
  98, 121; and violence, 97
Rich, Adrienne, xiii, 2, 4, 11, 18,
  19, 57, 73–74, 78, 89, 141n1
Riffaterre, Michael, 110–12
Riley, Denise, 98n3
Robinson, Lillian, 59–60
Rukeyser, Muriel, xvin3
Russo, Mary, 23
Ruthven, K. K., 58, 66–67, 71n9

Said, Edward, 97
Salusinszky, Imre, 88
Sand, George, 42–47, 127, 142n3
Sappho, 69, 114
Schenck, Celeste, 142n2
Schor, Mira, 146
Schor, Naomi, xviin8, 26n2, 48, 59,
  81–82
Sedgwick, Eve Kosofsky, 1, 24,
  30n21, 59
Segrest, Mab, 3
Self; authorization, 129–30, 131–
  32; consciousness, xii, 89–90,
  125; fictionalization, 113; naming,
  99n8; representation, x, 2, 17, 61,
  98, 99n8, 133–35; resistance, 15–
  16
Separatism, 67, 71n9, 112
Sexual difference, 12–13, 78–80,
  105. *See also* Difference

Shaw, Peter, 104
Shopping, 139–41
Showalter, Elaine, 14, 26n2, 34, 57
Simon, Kate, 124
Slavery, 108, 109–10, 113
Smelik, Anneke, 27n4
Smith, Barbara; "Toward a Black
  Feminist Criticism," 2, 84–86
Smith, Bessie, 89
Smith, Valerie; *Self-Discovery and
  Authority in Afro-American Nar-
  rative*, 108–10, 113
Snitow, Ann, 2
Solomon-Godeau, Abigail, 29n20
Sophocles; *The Philoctetes*, 102–
  103, 115, 116, 117. *See also* Phi-
  loctetes
Spectacle, 23, 24, 25
Spillers, Hortense, 81
Spivak, Gayatri, 2, 18, 27n7, 83,
  96, 114
Staël, Germaine de; *Corinne or It-
  aly*, 68–69
Steedman, Carolyn; *Landscape for a
  Good Woman*, 3, 128
Stern, Daniel, 127
Stern, Henry J., 118
Stimpson, Catharine R., 98n1
Structuralism, 9, 13, 40, 55
Subject; of deconstruction; 81; fe-
  male, 13, 75, 125, 126; feminist,
  78, 132; of language, 9; male au-
  tobiographical, 125; in power, 68,
  71n8; social, 20; of theory, 21
Suleiman, Susan, 26n2, 79–80

Teaching, 15, 18–19, 38–47, 54–55,
  121–41; feminist, xii–xiii, 33, 39,
  40–42; and students, 39, 40, 116,
  122, 124; tactics, 18–19, 41–42;
  writing, 133–35

I realized that when I write I collect my collection is memoir run back on to self by making a collage — (surrealistic pod ")